Ordinary Trauma

Ordinary Trauma

A MEMOIR

Jennifer Sinor

THE UNIVERSITY OF UTAH PRESS

Salt Lake City

The Defiance House Man colophon is a registered trademark of
the University of Utah Press. It is based on a four-foot-tall Ancient
Puebloan pictograph (late PIII) near Glen Canyon, Utah.

21 20 19 18 17   1 2 3 4 5

Library of Congress Cataloging-in-Publication Data
Names: Sinor, Jennifer, 1969- author.
Title: Ordinary trauma : a memoir / Jennifer Sinor.
Description: Salt Lake City : The University of Utah Press, [2017]
Identifiers: LCCN 2016030086
ISBN 9781607815372 (pbk. : alk. paper) | ISBN 9781607815389 (ebook)
Subjects: LCSH: Sinor, Jennifer, 1969- | Sinor, Jennifer, 1969—Family. |
    Psychic trauma in children. | Children of military personnel—Psychology.
    | Psychologically abused children--United States—Biography.
Classification: LCC CT275.S521765 A3 2017 | DDC 616.85/21083—dc23 LC
record available at https://lccn.loc.gov/2016030086

"The Bucket" contains text that has been revised since its previous publication in
Jennifer Sinor, *The Extraordinary Work of Ordinary Writing: Annie Ray's Diary* (2002). Parts
of "The Fall" first appeared in *Bellingham Review*. Parts of "The Fish" first appeared
in *Fourth Genre*, a publication of Michigan State University Press. Parts of "The
Skates" first appeared in *Under the Sun*.

While this is a work of nonfiction, some names have been changed.
Printed and bound in the United States of America.

For my parents.

1

The Bucket

Late April 1969. For the past few weeks, purple spiderwort and phlox have begun to appear along the cactus-rimmed roads of Kingsville, Texas, a naval town. The flowers have risen open-faced and ready after a short, mild winter, one noticeable only to the locals. Within several months, somewhere in the hot middle of summer, the roads will fill with June bugs the size of small mammals. Those who have lived in Kingsville for at least one summer already know that when driving these June-bugged roads, they need to turn the radio up to drown the sound of bodies crunching beneath the tires. But this comes later. Now it is spring. And in rhythm with the rest of the natural world, the obstetrics ward of the Kingsville County Hospital is filled with women giving birth.

A man hurries into a waiting room. Tree-tall and just as narrow, he wears a dark suit with a thin, black tie. The fluorescent lighting draws out the red in his hair, setting the crown aflame. Not stopping at the registration desk or to check the hospital floor plan posted near the elevator, he moves through the halls with the precision of a surgeon. It is his second visit to the hospital that day. Only a few hours before, having made sure his wife was safely in the hands of the doctors, he had rushed home to shower, shave, and change from his jeans and t-shirt. When his first child came into the world, he wanted to be wearing a suit. Now, shaving cream still clinging to the lobes of his long ears, he returns, suited, and finds a place in the waiting room with the other fathers. The total trip has taken only a little over an hour. What he doesn't know is that the waiting has just begun.

HOURS LATER, THE young man still sits in the windowless room of the Kingsville County Hospital, shaving cream wiped from his ears. Nurses flit by offering the occasional cup of coffee or a few words of encouragement. Once or twice they assure him the doctor will be out to see him soon. But still he waits.

Other new fathers have appeared and disappeared throughout the afternoon, passing out cigars as a way to feel a part of things. Cheap tobacco presses against his chest. A man used to being in charge, only recently released from his tour of duty in Vietnam where he had served as a legal advisor, he does not wait well. He also has an innate distrust of doctors, perhaps because they possess a knowledge that he does not. All afternoon he has struggled with himself not to move beyond the swinging doors and take the scalpel into his own hands. While he has delivered calves and colts as a young boy on his family's farm in Nebraska, he knows nothing about delivering a baby. Even given his own ignorance, though, he realizes that a wait this long is not good. The next time a nurse walks by, he tells himself, he will demand to see the doctor.

He considers calling his parents who still live in Cozad, Nebraska, but decides against it. Long distance is expensive; only bad news justifies the cost. Because he and his wife haven't lived in Kingsville long enough to make the kind of friends who appear at the hospital with brown paper bags full of food, he rarely looks up when someone enters the room. Instead, he rereads *National Geographic*. Occasionally he walks to the nursery to make sure that his first child hasn't arrived in this world without his knowledge. The same babies sleep there every time, bound tightly in hospital blankets. As afternoon pushes into evening, he stops imagining what his child might look like.

THE DOCTOR ARRIVES. He bursts into the waiting room, having not even taken the time to change his blood-soaked scrubs. Sweating and out of breath, it is as if the doctor has been the one in labor. The young man—stunned by the material fact of his wife's blood—finds himself rehearsing over and over the patterns created by the mint-green fabric and dried blood on the doctor's smock. Clouds, flowers, buildings, snakes. At least here is something he can hold onto. Because of the sweating and the breathing and the general chaos the doctor brings with him into the tiny waiting room, the young man does not absorb every word the doctor says, but by highlighting the key terms he comes to understand that things have gone badly in the delivery room. So badly in fact that he must now choose to save either his wife or what could be or would have been his daughter.

The dark suit seems painfully out of place. News like this, he worries, should be met less formally. It could appear to someone on the outside, a bystander, one of the cigar-laden new fathers, that he has come to the hospital prepared to mourn.

Faced with the possibility of losing the woman that he loves, the young man chooses his wife. He lets the daughter go.

WHAT IS HAPPENING in the delivery room now that the doctor has returned with the father's decision? The doctor's patient has long been unconscious. Perhaps from the drugs, or the pain, or the loss of blood, she has slipped into a comatose state. The baby is wedged in the birth canal, doubled up, her rear end first. The doctor is not able to say for sure what has gone wrong. He reviews his decisions, questions his choices, and considers the options that remain. At moments the delivery room has been noisy and panicked. There were the pain-filled screams of the then-conscious woman, the shouted commands of the doctor, and the urgent questions from the nurses. Now, as the same doctor studies the rear end of the baby and considers how best to remove the body, it is quiet. The baby is a test question he works to get right.

In the end, he chooses to fracture. With confidence born from a decision reached, he breaks her collarbone swiftly and in so doing severs the nerves in her neck. No longer worried about the fact that the umbilical cord has wrapped around her windpipe, denying her oxygen for long periods of time, he pulls the broken body out with forceps.

Father waiting, mother unconscious, the darkened body of the fetus is dropped into a bucket on the floor and shuttled across the linoleum into an adjoining room.

The doctor begins suturing the woman's tears.

SOMETIME LATER, THE wounds almost closed, blood loss stemmed, the color returns to the woman's cheeks like sun on a field. Nurses shuffle in and out of the room, carrying trays and charts and rubber gloves and tools. Some help to stitch the woman back together at the seams; others begin to scrub the tables and floor. Sometime after six p.m. an older, green-scrubbed doctor who has recently begun his shift walks through the adjoining room and sees the bucket holding the discarded baby on the floor. At first, he does not know that it is a baby. He just sees a form. Intuition, experience, hope, or the universe nevertheless causes him to stop. He makes a choice. From what will forever be known as The Dead Baby Bucket, the doctor pulls the baby out. Though bloody and broken and blue from lack of heat and oxygen, it is breathing. The dead baby breathes.

2

The Nurse

At the curb of the Kingsville County Hospital, the nurse handed her the tiny bundle wrapped in pink. The blanket concealed the bandages that held her daughter's collarbone in place. With only her face showing, her baby looked undamaged. Heat pulsed from the asphalt around the running Chevrolet, igniting her stockinged legs. When she had walked out of the hospital, it was as if she were being born again, this time as a mother of a daughter who should not be alive, the mother of a miracle. She had been in the hospital for so long, waiting for both body and daughter to heal, that she had forgotten the sting of the Texas sun, even in May. She welcomed the heat, though, turned her face into the sun. Pain, she had come to understand in the last few weeks, made you firm in the knowledge that you were alive.

The nurse had insisted on putting her in a wheelchair while she carried the baby. She felt silly being wheeled by her husband down the narrow sidewalk while others, in particular an older man leaning on a cane, made their way without conveyance. And she wanted to hold her child.

At the curb, the nurse relinquished the bundle, her daughter quiet for the first time all morning, probably asleep. In the months to follow, her husband would say that all their daughter did was sleep, eat, and scream. He was right. She would argue their daughter mostly screamed. She knew how her own body felt after the traumatic birth, and here was her broken baby wrapped in an elaborate sling. Fierceness rose in her belly, and she set her jaw, determined to chart an easier course.

"Let her cry," the nurse said, just before she closed the door on the Chevrolet.

Her husband was loading the trunk with the suitcases and rafts of blankets.

"Pardon?"

The nurse, who was older than she had first realized, maybe fifty, with tightly curled hair and cat-shaped glasses that slipped from the bridge of her nose, pointed to her daughter. "Let her cry. Check her diaper, look for pins that might be poking her, make sure she is fed, and then leave her in the crib, walk around the block, then walk around again."

She squinted her eyes against the sun and tried to find some sense in what the nurse had said, but before she could ask again, her husband arrived in the driver's seat.

"Ready?" he asked.

And she nodded.

3

The Sandbox

My father served in the military for more than twenty years. A naval lawyer, one of the first in the newly established JAG Corps, he specialized in maritime law. He joined the navy in 1966 in an effort to avoid the draft. Having recently finished law school at the University of Nebraska, he started Officer Candidate School and awaited the first set of orders.

My parents and I moved to Hospital Point Housing on the Pearl Harbor Naval Base in 1972 when I was three. Named for the hospital that once perched on the edge of the harbor, Hospital Point was a cemetery long before it became military housing. On December 7, 1941, the hospital burst with wounded bodies, sailors burned on their arms and legs from swimming through the flaming harbor. As a child, I was only dimly aware that the oily-black water lapping at my feet concealed an unknown number of bodies and sunken ships. I walked past the concrete memorials with their bronze plaques, traced my fingers along the raised lettering.

In my yard, bushes dipped and bent in the offshore breezes, oleander and plumeria, hedges of hibiscus and ti, coconut palms, date, mango trees with leaves that glinted like a thousand mirrors. And the flowers: electric pinks, reds, and purples of hanging torch ginger, heliconia, jacaranda, bird of paradise. Bougainvillea climbed the house, the lanai, the tennis court fence nearby. Standing beneath the white plumeria in the corner of my yard, I thought the world perfumed and vibrant, a festival of birdsong.

I was less sure what to do with the destruction. Out past the plumeria and near where the Chinese banyan let down its roots like a woman her hair, cement pedestals remained buried in the long grass, marking the foundation of the once-busy hospital. Amputated steel cables and years of crumbling neglect made running along this wide, concrete beam possible. On walks with my parents around the neighborhood, we would often end up in this field, in wreckage. A hospital without walls, floors, nurses, or stretchers, it sank into grass withered brown by the Hawaiian sun.

Only now do I see the irony found in the fact that we arrived in a housing area named for a hospital just at the moment my parents no longer had need for one. I am told that the first long year after I was born, living in Fairmont, Minnesota, where we moved after my birth, was one of constant screaming. I can only imagine my mother holding this wailing baby wrapped in gauze. The doctors had set my collarbone and felt hopeful about nerve regeneration, but they had less confidence in my mental abilities. Deprived of oxygen for too long, my brain was most certainly damaged. My parents waited for my body to seize and spiral, my eyes to roll white. They never unwrapped the complicated bandages that ran from shoulder to belly for fear of being unable to reassemble me.

Bodies, though, heal. By the time we arrived in Hawaii, no stranger could have read traces of trauma on my skin. My younger brother, Scott, was born the first Christmas after our arrival, and, with the demands made by a new baby, the difficulty of the past several years was forgotten.

That my backyard held both a tire swing and a bomb shelter did not seem unusual. The bomb shelter had existed for so long the earth had grown over it and grass carpeted the sides. Like the bougainvillea and hibiscus, it rose from the dirt.

One afternoon, when I was not yet five, I dug in the sand wearing only my bathing suit bottoms, my chest as brown as my hands, my brown hair bleached almost blonde by the sun. All around me mynahs chattered and plumeria bobbed like buoys on a sea of green. I noticed little of this as I dug, only felt the sand grow cooler the deeper I pushed my shovel.

Amid the smells and color, the clanks and whistles of the harbor, two older boys came up the flank of the bomb shelter behind me, both of them toe-headed and bronzed. I recognized them from the house down the street. One held a baseball glove in his hand but no ball. For a moment, I wondered if he had lost it in the sand.

"Looky here," the taller one said, standing between me and the sun and throwing a shadow across the castles I had been making. "Is it a girl or a boy?"

I stopped building and looked up. They were tall, thin, eel-like.

"A boy," the second decided, waving the empty baseball glove in the air. "A boy, a boy, a boy," he chanted, kicking sand over my feet and blocking the view of my house.

"I'm a girl," I said, standing, upset by their destruction of my castles more than at their taunts.

"Where's your top then, girly? Or do you like being naked?"

I had no answer; it had never occurred to me that I was naked. I stood. The sand fell from the creases in the cotton fabric of my bathing suit. I looked down.

"You must like being naked," the gloved one said again, "or maybe you wish you were a boy."

The two circled around me, fingers flicking the ends of my hair and sending rivulets of sand down my bare shoulders. On top of a bomb shelter that slept like a giant beneath me, I stood in the sun, solid in the knowledge that I had done something wrong.

Before they could find more fault with me, I broke from their gaze and galloped down the grassy sides toward home. When I looked back from the safety of my porch, I could no longer see the boys. What I could see was the shelter itself, a mound of grass with a door on the front made of wood and painted brown. It was through this door, narrow like a tooth, that we would enter when the bombs fell.

4

The Boots

At the age of eight, he spent most nights poring over the worn Sears catalog, one of the only books in the farmhouse, looking for a new pair of boots. He had never had a new pair of anything, had worn the overalls handed down from his older brothers, learned to cuff his jeans. But the corn had paid well, so he dog-eared pages and dreamt of leather every night, his mother in the kitchen scouring the cast-iron pan.

Holes plagued the seams of the boots he wore then, tears that seem to grow larger every day. When he checked the irrigation canals in the morning, the dew seeped into his socks, leaving the arch of his foot wrinkled and white. He vowed to keep a thick coat of polish on his new boots and to avoid brambles and brush. And he begged his parents until they relented. On a Friday in early fall, his mother mailed the order form. He marked the day on the calendar that hung in the kitchen and began the wait.

The package arrived when he was at school, a wide box wrapped in brown paper. The boots had been sent to his father and remained unopened; when he got home he used his pocketknife to cut the string. Resting in the box like two black kittens, the boots nestled in white tissue paper. He noted, with satisfaction, the corded laces, the plastic binding at the tips. Nothing frayed, nothing worn, all shiny and new.

And too small. He could tell as soon as he tried to jam his foot into the first boot. He loosened the bootlaces, pulled his white sock tight against his heel, and tried again. This time he succeeded in getting his foot into the boot, but his toes were bent and already aching. He could just make out his big toe bulging against the leather.

"We have to send them back," his mother said, as he hobbled around the kitchen table trying to conceal the problem.

"No," he insisted. "They just need breaking."

He could not imagine waiting more weeks for a new pair to arrive, and he worried his father would change his mind if the boots proved a hassle. He walked on the outside edges of his feet, pulled his toes in, looked at his mother as if to say, "see."

She conceded because there wasn't time in her day to argue with an eight-year-old about footwear, and it saved a return trip to town. He spent much of the first day sitting on a chair in the living room, swinging his boots while he listened to the radio; his feet didn't ache as much when he wasn't standing on them.

That afternoon his uncle came to the house for dinner.

"Let me see those boots, Red," he said, a wink toward the kitchen where his mother stood.

When he hobbled across the room toward him, his uncle added, "Seem a bit tight, don't they?"

He shook his head, drew in his toes, and kept to the shadows of the living room. After dinner, he sat on the porch with his uncle, the boots off, toes free, moon riding high in the still-warm sky. His boots rested at the edge of the porch, the eyelets surveying the fields.

"You know, I once had some boots like that," his uncle said, "didn't feel just right on my feet." His uncle sat in a straight-backed chair, pitched precariously on two legs, and spit sunflower seeds into the hard-packed yard. "Tell you what I did. I cut the toe box off, just took it right off, gave my feet the room they needed."

The thought of cutting the leather made the boy's stomach clench. At his uncle's words, he reached for the boots and pulled them close, buried his face in the leather that smelled of saddle and hay. He and his uncle sat for a long time in the darkness, the muffled sounds from the house barely reaching them above the cicadas. After a while, his father joined them on the porch, chawing tobacco rather than sunflower seeds; he agreed with his own brother's suggestion. "That's the only way makes sense," he said.

The boy made the first cut that night, the leather marred so easily, the boots not a day old. Where his father and uncle couldn't see him, he took the future into his hands. He tried to make the cut even, but he was unskilled and the leather, thick. That winter he walked to and from school with wet and frozen feet.

5

The Chair

My father's father was sold as an apprentice at the age of twelve to a maverick oil company. He took a train from Kentucky to Texas to learn to weld in oil wells and rigs even before his voice cracked. A narrow boy, he could fit in tight places, often upside down, to weld metal fittings so the rig could keep hauling black gold from the ground. He learned to tolerate enormous amounts of heat and pain. Working intimately with the arc inches away, no room to move, he would settle into the earth as into a chair, the welder's flame, hot and blue, his constant source of light.

6

The Needles

At the age of ten, his father gives him no curfew, no boundaries, no rules, in exchange for doing the work of a man.

But he isn't a man.

He stands with his older brother, Bill, at the front of the barn, their Nebraska farmstead stretching in all directions around them, wind kicking wheat chaff and corn pollen into the air. It is 1950 and their father has left them in charge of the pigs. Their father is a man they know best from the back, one who often turns, as he does that day, and leaves them in the dark coolness of the barn with a job to be done. In this case: corral the small brood of pigs so they can be injected with a vaccine in their rumps. The vaccine and syringes sit on the large post near the corral, fresh and ordered. He and Bill have not been alone in the barn fifteen minutes before they fill the tubes with water and convert expensive syringes into squirt guns.

For the next several hours, the two of them scramble the haystacks and scale the loft ladder, all the while pumping the tiny plungers and releasing long, cool streams of irrigation water. The planked floor soon turns to muck as the water mixes with the remnants of manure and mice. Every now and then, one of them is hit by a jet of water and takes a fantastic tumble behind the hay rake or into a nearby and empty stall. They re-enact scenes from the Western they saw in town the week before, taking turns playing the bad guy or the Indian, unaware of the passage of time. Well away from the house where their mother prepares an early supper of boiled chicken and gravy, they play unchecked.

When the first syringe breaks, they examine the shards of glass only for a moment before they secure another water pistol from the shrinking stack of tubes and begin again, now shooting one syringe while shoving a second deep into the pocket of their overalls for back up. Several more syringes break from the rough landings and the moments when they misjudge the depth of the hay. Within thirty minutes, the boys are soaking wet, their hair clumped in chunks and framing their sunburned faces, the collars on their white t-shirts slack around their necks. The syringes meant for shooting into thick-skinned pigs, every one of them, lie broken at their feet.

Before their father returns that evening from town, he and Bill bury the shards of glass and useless plungers in the bushes that run alongside the farmhouse. The hole they dig is not deep, but the branches are low and conceal the uneven ground. They wash for supper.

"How did the pigs go?" their father asks, sinking his teeth into a cob of corn grown in his own fields. Because his mouth is full, the question arrives muddled, but the boys know what he has said.

They admit they weren't able to finish the job.

"Why not?" their father asks, grabbing another cob from the buttery stack.

"We lost the syringes," he says, and looks quickly at Bill with the unspoken threat not to contradict.

"Lost? I don't understand?" The once bustling, clinking table no longer moves.

"We don't know." He rushes now. "We were out there, and the pigs were giving us trouble, and they were pushing on the gate, Bill tried to secure it, and Jerry wasn't around, and Bill tried again, and then the box wasn't there, maybe a pig did something to it, and we couldn't find them. We looked but—"

"Find them," his father says, and the matter is closed, like a barn door. Only the squeak of kernels torn from the cob remains.

Which is how, in the waning hours of daylight, he and Bill find themselves scouring the reaches of the farm looking in vain for syringes they know lie broken and buried not twenty feet from the dinner table. At some point, he begins to believe the syringes are only lost, misplaced in a moment of inattention. He begins to believe the lie that he has told, the story he has invented to save him from his father's belt. He searches the entire night.

—

7

The Bushes

The same two boys, still blonde but taller, who had found me on the bomb shelter when I was four now stood in my yard. In the intervening year, they had paid me little attention, allowed me to swing on my tire swing without comment as they blazed by on their banana-seated bicycles, the wind lifting their hair. But not that day. That day, out of boredom or curiosity, they found me in the front yard (or maybe already in the bushes) and turned their gaze again on my body.

Did they ask me to take down my pants? Did they threaten? I want them to raise their hands with sticks clenched tightly, sticks they have found under the shower tree, bendable and whip-like. I want them to say, "Take your pants down. Show us you're a girl." I want them to say, "We will beat you." I want them to say, "Do what we say or else." But in my memory I stood between the bushes and my house, the wooden siding at my back, red ants running the bridges of my shoeless feet, and pulled my cotton pants to my ankles without a single word.

Clouds passed over the sun and for a moment shadow consumed the yard. Above us, the palm trees clicked an undersea ballad, the ends of their fronds brown and brittle. I stood half-undressed.

Because my shirt barely covered my stomach, the shadow tickled in places rarely reached. The boys pointed their sticks, or they thrust their hips, or maybe they turned, already bored by the nakedness of a five year old. I couldn't flee, either because they blocked the escape or because my underwear would trip me or because I didn't want to. My eyes were down. I could see their bare feet, the red dirt between their toes, smell the sweat of their bodies. They pushed toward me, and I thought to scream.

But when I opened my mouth, the scream came from beyond the bushes, outside my body, from the sky itself, now bright and cloudless. I closed my mouth but the screaming continued.

"Get out! Get out!" the sky thundered. And the two boys were plucked from the hedge, leaving the hibiscus leaves shaking at the edges of where they once stood. "How dare you!"

Anger vibrated from my father's body, tall against the sky, taller than the palm trees, the plumeria, the house, sending bolts into the air. He held his hands high above his head, open and thrashing, ready to bring the sky crashing down. Grabbing the boys, one in each hand, he hoisted them into his arms where they dangled helplessly.

"What the hell are you doing?"

Because my head was down, already pulling my underwear up, I could not say where his words were directed, whether he was screaming at me or the two boys. Ants bit my instep and heat climbed my face.

Without a sound, my father turned with the boys and bore them across the lawn. I watched his retreating back, two bodies caught in his iron grip, and remained in the leafy dark, wooden boards pressed against my spine.

8

The Pig

Emotions, my father told me growing up, only get in the way. They do not allow you to think. They prevent you from doing what you need to do. I believed him. I saw the way complete strangers responded to his calm authority in the hardware store or the grocery aisles. He was tall and strong and never wrong. As a child, it did not occur to me that my tears awoke something in his body he would sooner forget. That sorrow triggered anger because it could not be contained. To this day, my father walks out of the room at the end of most movies—whether the battle has been won or lost. It could be because he finds the aftermath less interesting than the conflict, but I have often wondered if it's the emotion of the denouement he would prefer to avoid.

When my father was young, he was given a pet pig, perhaps to teach him responsibility or animal husbandry. In my imaginings, the pig is Wilbur, though in fact I am sure his pig was far from sweet and pink and clean. I have lived near pigs, and they are enormous, rooting animals, who cry like humans caught in pain when all they want is food. But this pig, his pig, must have been adorable. It won his boyhood heart.

The pig followed him on his chores like a dog. Whether milking cows, driving the combine, moving hay, he brought the pig, who came along, always watching, waiting for a bit of bread or bite of carrot that he kept in his overalls pocket. At night, he curled up with the pig in the hayloft under the Nebraska sky, stars as thick as snow, the Milky Way like a road leading to a different life.

One day, his father came to him and said it was time to slaughter the pig. It was meant for the market, its path chosen long before birth. And it was up to my father to kill the pig, just as it was he who had cared for it. There were no questions, just, yes sir. On that same day? A day later? Perhaps on Saturday when his mother did the wash and had boiling water standing and ready for use. There he was, that day or later, but only ten, barely big enough to lift the ball peen hammer and bring it crashing down.

He is still there, in the backyard of the farmhouse, plains stretching away like childhood, the scream of the pig cut loose on the wind.

9

The Dog

In the days right before we left Pearl Harbor and headed for the next duty station—days in which our household goods had already been shipped across the Pacific and we lived in empty quarters on rental furniture supplied by the navy—my parents rescued a poodle they found wandering the beach. At home, Scott and I promptly named the poodle Peanut and chased him around the empty house.

Within a few hours of being home, though, Peanut had snapped at all of us, tiny little nips that made me cry. I realize now my parents never meant to keep him, biter or not, but at the time I thought he was ours. In a few days, a plane would take us back to the mainland. Peanut couldn't come. My parents put an ad in the paper, and soon he was gone.

Soon we were gone, too, off to Virginia and a tour of duty at the Pentagon, but the memory of Peanut haunted me. That something could so easily be abandoned, not to an empty beach but to the unknown; a nip here and bite there and you were left behind.

10

The Rock

Lava, however, comes with us. A chunk taken from the slopes of Mauna Kea, the home of Pele, Goddess of Fire. My parents had flown to the Big Island with our next-door neighbors, the Rices, just before we had left the islands. Mr. Rice had piloted the tiny plane, plunging and soaring above the Molokai Channel until my mother, pregnant with my second brother, Bryan, vomited into a brown paper bag. While Scott and I stayed with a babysitter, they spent the weekend hiking the volcanoes and soaking in Queen's Bath, a pool made of lava and adorned with ferns.

Pele lives in the Halemaumau Crater of Mauna Kea, the highest mountain in the world measured from the floor of the sea, and she curses anyone who takes lava from the flanks of her volcanoes. Known as earth-eating woman, the devourer, she creates and destroys at a whim. Locals offer rocks wrapped in ti leaves along with their prayers to appease her violent tendencies and capricious nature. Goddess of fire, quick to anger, her lava pulses down her slopes, sparing none.

My parents decide to place their black chunk of *a'a* on the bookshelf in the basement of our new house. Sharp and pointed, not smooth like *pahoehoe*, the jagged piece of rock pricks my palm; the surface, sheen and shadow.

Little light exists for either the lava or the rest of us in our new house, a brick split-level that sits at the end of a cul-de-sac amid a forest of deciduous trees. Even in the winter, when the branches are bare of leaves, the house feels threatened. The two picture windows, one in the living room and one in the dining room, cannot let enough sun in to heat the rooms. Because there is a fireplace downstairs, we spend most of the winter in the basement, the bright orange shag carpet stretching to the wood paneling on all four walls. Having spent the past four years in Hawaii surrounded by sunshine, it feels as if we are living inside the earth.

With our arrival in Virginia, my father disappears. Each weekday morning, he heads to the Pentagon, sometimes in a carpool, sometimes on the Metro, always in the dark. At night his footfalls ring against the brick announcing his return. Out the window, I cannot see him beneath the trees and the sunless sky, but I know what he is wearing, the same uniform he wore every day for twenty years, the one my mother irons at night while I watch *Wonder Woman*, a can of Niagara starch nearby, and the hot smell of the iron filling the air. Every three days she washes another load, first checking the pockets for the black ballpoint pens issued by the government. Every three days she presses deep creases back into the polyester.

Those first months, we seem to move in darkness, hands held out in front of us hoping to touch something familiar. Instead of the scent of plumeria when I open the door, there's the smell of a thousand rotting leaves. My mother rubs her pregnant belly, unable to imagine caring for three children. And my father ducks his head carefully before getting off the Metro, already deep underground in the Pentagon.

When my father is home, those few minutes between dinner and bed, he towers over me while I do my homework. At the Pentagon, men do what he says. At home, his daughter cries over subtraction.

His khaki pants brush the back of my chair, static electricity snapping the ends of my hair.

He jabs his finger on a problem. "It's all right there," he says. "Think it through."

The numbers blur through my tears, and I hold the thick pencil at an angle, not ready to write. My mother loads the dishwasher in the kitchen, the sharp ting of glassware and plates. The sound of the water running in the sink lets me know she's not coming to the table.

"Why are you making it so hard, Jennifer?"

Impatience sets his lips.

Big drops of water hit the math sheet and smear the pencil marks.

"Crying isn't going to help," he says. Then he unbends his body and yanks the chair next to me closer so he can sit. The action startles me, and I jump.

Frustration pulses from his body. I know if I look up I will see that his hazel eyes have dimmed to black points. His forearms lock on the table, the hair on his arms red. His temper can ignite at any moment, can choose any target or flare at anything in its path. Part of the reason I don't mind my father's long hours is that it means I don't have to navigate the minefield of his moods.

"Is it seventeen?" I ask, still crying.

He rises. "I don't have time for guessing. When you have done the problem correctly, you call me. Until then, not a word."

I have an entire page of problems to finish before I can go to bed.

As soon as he is gone, taking his smoldering rage with him, I wish him back again. I want to please him, earn his favor. But he leaves me at the table and heads to his bedroom to change. Moments later the radial arm saw spins to life and severed two-by-fours fall to the ground.

"Eighteen," I say to the now-empty room. "It's eighteen."

11

The House

My father is a monster. He crawls around the living room on all fours and grabs for our legs, growling. "I'm going to get you." With a swipe, he seizes my ankle and pulls me toward his gnashing teeth. I laugh and struggle to break free. His hands are iron. Pry his thumb and index finger and the other three hold; pull those from your ankle and the thumb and finger return like a vise. Scott attacks from the side and is quickly taken to the floor. I dive for my father's belly, pushing my fingers into the soft folds, hoping to topple the man who remains on all fours like a house.

"Rarrhh!" he cries, up on his knees, flailing his hands, looking for another ankle or arm.

"Get his hands! Get his hands!" Scott yells.

And I try, try to hold a hand as broad as my stomach while he moves to tickle my knees, my thighs, under my arms.

"Help, me!" I gulp between laughs to Scott, who is busy fighting his own hand, my father's head down, taking the two of us to the ground.

Soon I wet my pants, a squirt of urine leaving a wet place on my underwear that grows cool in minutes. But I don't stop. Out of breath and sore from being tickled, Scott and I mount a second attack as my father hunkers down on the carpet, protecting his face, moving toward us. He sweeps his arm like the beam of a lighthouse, while we scream and holler, "Time out!"

He stops, raises his head, checks to see who is hurt; Scott and I sit in the corner heaving and laughing.

"Be a monster, Daddy. Again, again."

12

The Bed

It is late September, a night we return home from an inexpensive dinner out. Scott and I sit in the back seat of the car, drawing imaginary lines on the vinyl and demanding that the other stay on their side. Even when we escalate the battle with pushing, a redrawing of the imaginary line, and then a skirmish between feet, we garner little attention from the front.

My parents aren't listening. As my dad pulls into the carport and turns the engine off, he looks over at my mother.

"Is it time?" he asks.

Because of his tone, I stop messing around and turn to the front. Is that fear I hear in my father's voice, that edge, that hesitation?

My mother sits unnaturally straight in her seat, her breath coming regularly, her hand resting on her stomach. Every now and then she reaches a bit higher, sits even taller.

"Yes," she says, and we are sent inside to pack clothes.

Only now looking back do I think of what the birth of a child might mean for my father. Only now do I recognize the possibilities that both of them faced.

"DO YOU WANT to save your wife or your daughter?" Is it that time?

WHILE MY MOTHER is in labor, I stay with Diane, a girl a few years older than me whose father is also in the JAG. That night, Diane and I get ready for bed. My brother Scott is sleeping in the other room with Diane's younger brother, Dennis. There is a sense that at any moment my father will come and get us, will take us home and carry us to bed.

I have never slept away from home before, and while the initial idea had seemed like a good one to me, I am now less sure. When my brother Scott had been born, I had been three. I don't really remember when he was not a part of my life. But this baby is different. Whose hand will he hold? Where will he sit in the car? Squares have four sides, cards, four suits, the Sunshine family four members. Five seems awkward and uneven. Spending the night away starts to feel less like a party and more like punishment. When I return home, the new baby will be sharing my room.

For the first part of the night, we watch television on their black-and-white set. Television programming in Virginia is as dull as the sky above it. In Hawaii, we watched episodes of Kikaider, a Japanese show that featured a guitar-playing man who turned into the superhero, Kikaider, whenever trouble arose. I would sit in my father's lap and yell "get 'em, get 'em" when the blue-suited thugs we called the "Get 'Em Guys" tried to take Kikaider down. The show was in Japanese with poorly translated subtitles that I was too young to read. But the plot required no translation for a girl who lived amid battleships and jet fighters: a threat arises and the good guys prevail. Each episode seemed to include a young Japanese boy, not any older than I was, wandering the hills outside a village calling for his father. "Otosan! Otosama!" I could never understand why his father went missing each week, but when he cupped his hands over his mouth and yelled for his father I recognized something in his face.

At some point that night, I wet the bed, soaking through the cotton sheets and ruining the blankets. When she awakes, Diane screams, looking at me as if I have hit her rather than merely dampened her nightgown. She runs around the room wiping her legs, yelling, "Gross! Gross!" The wet spot turns the green sheets darker, a forest blooming in the middle of the bed. I sit in the sea of wet blankets, thinking someone must have poured water on the mattress. I do not know that Pele, the earth devourer, has arrived.

13

The Phone Call

The morning after I wet the bed, now dressed in shorts and t-shirt because I haven't packed a second nightgown, I sit at the table eating breakfast with Diane. The washing machine spins my clothes clean in the room just off the kitchen. Diane has forgiven me and offers to braid my hair into pigtails. I feel grateful for my bowl of corn flakes and Diane's smile. The phone rings and Diane's mother moves to answer it, her apron strings catching on my chair as she passes by. She stands at the wall, wiping her wet hands on her apron, her voice low and concerned. At one point she turns her back on us and covers the phone with her hand as she talks. Minutes into the call, she beckons me over.

"Your father," she says and hands the phone to me.

It's the first time I have ever talked with my father on the phone, one of the first times I have ever talked on the phone at all, and I take it reluctantly, the receiver feeling unbalanced and strange in my hands. My father's voice seems to rise from under an even greater weight, coming to me thin and distant. He speaks slowly, choosing words like he might a tool, deliberately.

"You have a baby brother," he says without suspense or cheer. I wait for more. Diane has turned in her chair and looks at me, grinning, eyebrows raised.

"A boy," I whisper to her, my hand over the mouthpiece as I have seen my mother do. Diane frowns. We had both wanted a little girl that we could dress up and adorn with plastic barrettes.

My father remains silent. Perhaps he, too, had wanted a daughter. "How's Mommy?" I ask. "Are you coming to get me?"

"She's fine," he says and then pauses again.

The washing machine lurches to a sudden stop after the spin cycle and silence fills the kitchen. I sink to the floor with the phone, the cord wrapped around my waist pulling me tight. My father is never at a loss for words.

"What's his name?"

"He doesn't have a name."

"Why?" I ask, knowing that we have been talking about names for months at this point.

"Something happened," he says.

I can tell by the way he speaks that I don't want to know, don't want to own whatever it is that makes his strong voice break. In the kitchen sink across the room, the tap drips onto the dishes piled from breakfast; Diane returns to her cereal, the box propped in front of her; her mother wrings a dish-cloth in her hands, eyes on the floor. I wait for my father to continue, holding the phone awkwardly to my ear, knowing nothing will be the same.

"There was an accident, a nurse, he was burned. He—"

"Is it okay?" I ask, unsure of what I even need to be all right, only wanting the reassurance that parents provide, the promise they make from the moment of birth never to drop, never to harm, always to hold.

"I don't know," he says. Words I have never heard him say before.

14

The Cats

There are also kittens, legions of tiny kittens birthed by the barn cats and not needed on the farm. His job was to get rid of them. Every few months, another batch. Rather than knot the entire litter in a sack and throw them into the Tricounty Canal like his father showed him, he drowned each kitten separately by holding its tiny head under the water in a barrel that stood outside the barn. One after another as the sun climbed the sky. The struggle, the clawing, then limp. He got to where he could do it without even looking, could attend to the cows in the nearby field at the same time.

It was a farm, he would say. Animals died. You had a duty to them. Sometimes that duty included putting them down. Acts of violence were ordinary, stacked up like so many pieces of white bread on a farm table, consumed without a thought.

And yet it seeps out, that violence. It doesn't stay under with the kittens nor is it left with the blood on the slaughtering stump. You are hit. You are asked to kill. And one day the violence becomes too much for your body to contain, your child's body, the one that has yet to hit puberty, the one that knows the work of a man more than the ramblings of a boy. Then it emerges like a tidal wave and takes everything with it.

As a child my father was known as "Red," a name his father continued to call him late into his life, even when his red hair faded to a chestnut brown. His hair, a beautiful shade according to my mother, separated him from his siblings and made him remarkable in the tiny town. His nickname was a point of pride, given to him by his father, a man who spoke only to criticize and then more often than not chose the belt over words, the nickname the only gift other than the one that replaced childhood with a plow and complete freedom.

RED, TAKE CARE of the cats.

IT ERUPTS. ONE night—years of caring for a pet pig and dead kittens already behind him—he confronted another boy, two cars, maybe alcohol, and a fight that like most fights had a complicated history. He leapt from the car he was driving, ran back to the boy in the other car, and drew his knife, held it to his neck, ready to cut the boy open. Kill the boy. The kitten. The pig. Friends stopped him, threw my father to the pavement and pried the blade from his hand. He does not remember any of it. Rage blacked him out, a wave flooding consciousness.

THE SAME HANDS that tried to drive a knife into a boy's throat, that held kittens under the water until they died, that knew the feel of a skull when it gives, rocked me to sleep as a baby, held me when I skinned my knee.

15

The Nurse

For two years after my youngest brother, Bryan, was born, my father called him George. "Come here, George," he would say, holding out his arms to his third child, then running his fingers through Bryan's softly curling hair. It wasn't exactly that my father couldn't remember his son's name or that there had ever been the chance that Bryan would be a George. Rather, my father called his third child George because, for a long time, it wasn't clear whether Bryan would live. Had he died he would have been named Morris, after my father.

Minutes after his birth, blood and mucous still covering his tiny limbs, lungs hardly accustomed to breathing air, Bryan was taken from the delivery room to the NICU at Bethesda Naval Hospital where newborns were washed and measured. There, a nurse left him in a basin in the sink while she went to the next room but not before pressing the scalding hot pedal instead of the pedal for the temperate water they used to bathe newborns. Bryan lost most of the flesh on the lower half of his body when less than an hour old. He spent the first few months of his life in continual and excruciating pain.

Why the nurse left the room, how she could have pushed the wrong foot pedal, how she could have misunderstood his screams are questions perhaps Pele can answer. My parents asked and then asked again. They were only told the nurse had been fired, let go that night, poor compensation for a baby born into flame. Numerous grafts eventually repaired the skin on Bryan's thighs and feet, though he screamed for months, holding his body board-straight. He slept in leg braces his first year because his legs had grown misshapen in the incubator. To prevent infection, my mother touched her baby with gloved hands through a hole in the side of an oxygen tent. For weeks, Bryan was not held, had no sense of a world outside of pain, forgot the smell of his mother.

16

The Sun

At Hospital Point, I remember one afternoon, not long after Scott had been born, riding with my mother in an open boat from the ferry dock near our house to the landing at Ford Island where we could shop at the "other" commissary and play in the brown fields. Wearing an orange life preserver meant for adults, I held her arm as the wooden boat headed into the harbor, gulls caterwauling in the air and the breeze thick with salt. The boat was a utilitarian beige, as were most things in the military, and filled with the blue uniforms of enlisted sailors on their way to work. I could taste the salt on my lips, see the rainbow swirls of oil curling alongside our boat.

Except for the motor and the gulls, the day was quiet. None of the sailors spoke. The only movement in the boat came from the pilot in the back who smoked a cigarette as he held the rudder in place. The day was hot and the sun blazed down. I could feel the heat radiate from my mother's body and the sun reflected planks of light off her white sundress. When I looked at her, I had to squint my eyes. She seemed to be aflame. I burrowed closer, the fabric of her skirt hot beneath my arm, her wrists slightly damp with perspiration. Beneath us the water rocked our tiny boat and the sailors scuffled their feet on the wooden floorboards. They held their eyes down, never lifted them, aware, too, that we rode to Ford Island with the sun as our passenger.

17

The Record

That first fall in Virginia, Bryan still in an oxygen tent in the hospital, I listen to the same record every night as I go to sleep: *Rudolph the Red-Nosed Reindeer*. My mother puts meals on the table. My father takes out the trash. I listen to Burl Ives, and no one mentions Bryan. Outside, the trees toss their branches in wind and a rainfall of acorns spatter the roof.

On school days, I walk down our road to the bottom of the hill where I stand on the busy street and voluntarily enter a bus, driven by a woman named "Grandma," that whisks me away from my mother. In the afternoon, I run up the hill to greet her.

When the teacher announces Show and Tell, I know I want to bring my Rudolph record. That morning, to keep it safe, I tuck Rudolph behind my back for the duration of the short trip to school. Around me chaos reigns. "Sit down!" Grandma yells, rubbing her hand up and down her blue knit pants, eyes in the mirror and not on the road. The smell of the heater mixes with the exhaust fumes and circles about our heads; I look out the window at the gray morning, more leaves on the ground than on the limbs of the trees we pass, feeling the stiff album behind me, close to my body.

When we arrive at school, everyone rises like a tide to leave. Kids in the aisle stay the exodus to allow their friends to cut in front. Those in the back yell at the others to "Move it!" And I, the new kid, wait for a break, a moment when I will not be noticed, to sneak into the aisle and down the rubber-treaded steps.

By the time I arrive at the classroom under its bright fluorescent lights and yellow desks clustered in learning pods, I realize I've forgotten Rudolph. My backpack is empty. I beg, but the teacher will not let me leave the classroom. After all, the bus is long gone, Grandma already headed for the high school and the older kids who start an hour after we do. "It will be there later," she assures, handing out purple dittoes still heavy with the smell of ink. "Don't worry." Given that it is October and the crib in my room, the one for my baby brother, remains empty, I take little comfort in her off-hand reassurance.

That afternoon, I stand first in line to board the bus in order to have a clean sweep of the seats before the other kids can get my record.

Nothing.

I sit down on the bench seat in the back while the bus fills with children whose names I don't know. As soon as the bus starts, a JPO stands up in front and yells for our attention. Grandma pulls out of the parking lot and into the street, causing the boy to wobble between the seats. Grabbing the pole near the stairwell, he spreads his legs further and lifts Rudolph over his head.

"Is this anyone's?" he calls out.

"Mine! Mine! Mine!" yell the other kids around me, waving their arms madly, grins as wide as their bell-bottoms stretching across their faces.

"It's mine. It's mine," they cry, laughing and pushing.

Panic seizes me. The moment of joy I experience when I see him wave my record is quickly replaced by fear. How will he know it is mine?

I stretch my arm as high as I can, hoping to outdo all those in front of me, trying to catch the JPO's eyes, and certain I will never hold that record again. What will I listen to at night while my parents huddle in the dining room whispering to each other? I have made no new friends at school, I eat with no one at lunch, remain silent in the small groups the teacher puts us into, but I know that record, know the angle at which Rudolph flies across the cover, its exact shade of blue, the length of the pause Burl Ives allows before "But do you recall the most famous reindeer of all." Amid the thick trees of Virginia and its endless dark, that record is home.

The JPO walks to the back of the bus and hands it to me, amid a chorus of "ohhs" and kids pretending to be disappointed.

Only when I get home do I learn that the record has been broken, probably by sitting against it, from, it seems, loving it too dearly. That night under the blankets I sing, "You know Dasher and Dancer and Prancer and Vixen," the thunk of each acorn, a crack on the roof.

18

The Sun

One day I come home from school and my mother says, "I have a surprise for you!"

The cold late-fall air chases me into the living room, bringing a few brown oak leaves to skitter across the entryway.

I think of ice cream, of candy, a new baby doll. Before I can guess, she says, "Someone is here."

"Diane!" I cry, neck craning around the bamboo screen, expecting to see my military friend swinging her legs from the couch.

"No," my mother says, disappointment in her voice. Bryan probably fills her every waking minute. That he doesn't fill mine registers the distance between us. She takes my backpack and heads toward the kitchen, already pulling the lunch box out, sudsy water in the sink waiting.

"Who?"

"Your brother!" she says, turning to face me, her eyes watery and bright under the kitchen light.

My first thought is of Scott, who is always home. I shake my head, not understanding, but then remember I have a second brother, the one we never talk about, the broken one.

We walk into my parents' room and my mother takes me to the bassinet that has been empty for several months. There, lying on white sheets, is my blonde-haired younger brother, legs in braces, head held in one position by firm pillows.

I don't feel love, don't even feel joy, but I do feel relief. At that moment, my mother tucking the yellow blanket she has crocheted for him around his tiny hands, her gestures quiet and confident, I realize the emptiness that has been occupying our house. I release a long, slow breath, note the curling hair at his neck. My mother's smile, her happiness, makes it clear to me that all is well, even if I hadn't known we were suffering.

19

The Pool

Because we cannot spend the summer in the cool of the basement, my parents discuss alternatives to the heat. In a move that is both like and unlike my father, he arrives home from work one afternoon with a used above-ground swimming pool strapped to the car. A great bargain, we discover. Because he grew up in a house with so little, my father loves a deal. Even if we can never eat twenty pounds of potatoes, he will buy that amount if it costs the same as three. Likewise, mixed in with our furniture from my parents' travels are pieces my father has pulled from a Dumpster on his way home. My father has an eye for quality as well as bargains, so few can tell which furniture rode a boat home from Hong Kong and which arrived in the backseat of the car.

We don't "need" a pool, but the deal is too good, so now we have one. He argues that central air conditioning will cost much more and we can simply cool off in the pool before we head to bed each night. My mother shakes her head and says nothing. She is trying to get grass stains out of the knees of Scott's pants.

Over the next few weeks, my father borrows our neighbor's backhoe and clears a level space beneath a cluster of oak trees. The dirt grows in a pile next to the house, a mountain of red that climbs toward the eaves. He needs to clear a space big enough for a pool that is twenty-five feet long and fifteen feet wide. The above-ground pool is oval-shaped with white metal sides and blue posts and lining. Scott and I stand nearby and watch the giant machine combing the earth like a dinosaur foraging for food. The backhoe shrieks when backing up, and we run behind the trees yelling that the monster is coming.

My father wants a cool pool and he gets an icebox. The giant oaks shade the water all day, so the pool is never warmed. As much as Scott and I love to swim, we can only remain in the water for short blocks of time and often have to run to the cement patio and lie in the sun. My mother jumps into the water while mowing the lawn to escape swarms of gnats around her head.

Once a week, we follow my father in a train around the oval pool to create a whirlpool. The cycloning water causes the sticks, leaves, and acorns—dropped from the surrounding forest—to surface where my father can skim the debris. His tall body pushes a path in the cold water that is not unlike the destroyers I used to watch moving up the channel at Pearl Harbor. The water seems to rush to get out of his way and his body generates a wake that splashes over the sides of the four-foot-high pool, hitting the ground in a water-fall of sound. Scott and I are quickly lifted from our feet as the whirlpool gains momentum. We are carried along in the current, the trees whipping by us. The inflated tires and plastic beach balls ride the storm with us, my family united for a moment in a giant swirling mass.

Except Bryan. He is too young to swim. Which is why, most afternoons, Scott and I play in the pool while Bryan sits on a small, wooden fan deck attached to the side of the pool. My father built the fan deck and stained it red to match the

dirt he cleared for the pool. The deck has a set of stairs my
parents can hoist to prevent us from accessing the pool when
they are not around. The steps are down when my mother is
outside with us. She is often skimming the pool, her brown
skin slicked with Hawaiian Tropic and shining in the sun.

Every night the whole family jumps into the pool before
bed. I fall asleep to the smell of chlorine on a pillow made
damp by my hair.

20

The Pennies

I sit with Bryan in the bedroom that we share, the crib against one wall, my twin bed against another, the dresser that doubles as a changing table covered in bars of Ivory soap impaled with diaper pins. It turns out I don't mind sharing my room. Bryan takes up little space, and at night I enjoy falling asleep to his ragged baby breaths.

Gathered at the wooden table my father made for me, we sit with my mother, who had been, only moments before, painting her toes, drawing the pink polish across each nail. Now she is gone, taking the bread from the oven, calling the sitter, stirring the soup.

She paints her toes now because she and my father are going out tonight and she cannot paint them in the car. Her long skirt won't allow her to bring her foot to the seat, a position she would never assume even if she could. In the car, I know, she will find the time to do her fingernails, position her hand on the armrest that separates her seat from my father's. Her nails will be shiny and bright when they arrive at the party.

Bryan and I remain at the table, neither of us noticing when the furnace ignites or the cat enters. I am counting pennies from an old Yuban coffee can that my mother has painted brilliant green with pale white and yellow flowers twisting around the sides. Spare change. The counting is something I often do, stacking the worn pennies in piles of tens and ordering them into ranks.

Each time I finish, I return the money to the can so that I can sort again later. All along the wooden top, I arrange rows of copper, dimes and nickels thrown to the ground. Ten, twenty, thirty, and, at a hundred, a dollar.

What I do know is that I have counted close to four dollars in change. What I am unsure of, even to this day, is whether I see Bryan drinking the nail polish remover. I do not want to lose my place in the count, of that I am clear. The pennies fixate. So much seems to depend on the rows. When my mother returns to the room, white Kleenex threaded in and out of her painted toes, she finds the wooden table covered in orderly piles, the floor around her spotted by rejected silver coins, and both the Yuban coffee can and the bottle of fingernail polish remover empty.

Shaking the empty bottle in the air, she cries, "Did he drink this?"

"I don't know," I answer. And that is maybe the truth.

Whisking Bryan up, my mother knocks the pennies to the ground. I remain in the room amid the spilled copper. Within fifteen minutes the ambulance arrives, the sirens disrupting the weekday afternoon. Not waiting for the medics to locate their boxes and tanks, my mother bundles Bryan in a blanket and grabs his medical record, rushing out to meet the EMTs who park on the steep driveway.

Hunched over my Holly Hobby diary that afternoon, in scrunched, barely-learned cursive, I name what I saw and failed to do. Or what I might have seen. Or what I didn't see but should have. I try to fasten the truth to the page. Then I lock the diary with a tiny, bronze key and stand at the picture window to wait for my mother to return.

When she enters, Bryan is asleep in her arms, and my father, not yet home from work.

"They pumped his stomach," she tells me as she sets her purse on the bench in foyer. When I say nothing, she continues, "It wasn't clear if he'd actually drunk anything, so they just did it."

Even the doctors can't tell me if I am to blame.

"I'm putting Bryan in his crib," she says, and carries him up the stairs. When she returns to the kitchen to start dinner, I run to the room where Bryan sleeps and stash the diary under my pillow. While I can't articulate it at the age of seven, this is the first time writing fails me. Truth can't be put into rows like pennies or captured with letters and a pen. I want to pin the world down, line it up, make it legible. But I can't even tell you to this day if I watched my brother drink the poison. Truth, what really happened, doesn't much matter. It's the shape of the story you carry—chosen, borrowed, or wrought—that determines the heft of your load. Those two years in Virginia, I saw no end to what was mine to bear.

A nip here, a sip there, and you would be left behind.

"Do you want to save your wife or daughter?"

The door to the bomb shelter is padlocked.

21

The Deck

Before the pool came the patio with its second-story deck. We built both in the spring, while the lava gathered dust in the basement and cherry blossoms burst like popcorn on the Washington Mall. My mother stowed the nail polish remover on the highest bathroom shelf, located the Crockpot, and put on her work gloves.

Over stew made with squares of meat and bone-white potatoes, my parents discussed the materials they would need for the deck, the possible structures and shapes. They wanted a place where we could sit and enjoy warmer weather. Given that our sun exposure had been reduced significantly since moving from Hawaii, we were all anxious to be outside. My parents did not call a contractor, didn't buy plans or consult with local builders. My mother made a sketch and my father got his tape measure out. Then we set to work.

By mid-May, the patio and deck were coming along. A concrete company poured the slab once the temperature remained consistently above freezing, which meant Scott and I could ride our bikes along its gritty surface. One afternoon, a week or so after the pad had been poured, my father stood under the high clouds in just a t-shirt and jeans as he framed the deck. He relied on two-by-sixes and long nails to carve a place in the air where we could enjoy the trees safe from the gnats and mosquitos. Each hammerfall echoed against the bricks of the house, ringing over and over. When he missed, he cursed the wood or the nails or one of us if we happened to be nearby. Our job was to hold boards for him, make sure the bubble in the level remained between the hair-thin lines. With each fall from the hammer, the board threatened to skitter and jump out of place.

My father complained, "Hold them still! Hold them still!" The bubble refused to remain in bounds. "Goddamnsonofabitch!"

His hands were scarred from misses; scratches and bruises lined the backs of his fingers and forearms. Still, he seemed happy in his work, as happy as my father ever seemed to be. He yelled and swore and grumbled about how nothing ever worked right, but I thought he enjoyed being outside, working with his hands.

My mother was not around. Or at least in my memory she was not around. Perhaps she was hauling dirt in the wheelbarrow or was making a run to the lumberyard down the street where she would sort through dozens of boards to find the kind my father liked, the ones without knots and bows, straight and true.

It was understood that we would work all day. With my father's schedule at the Pentagon, we only had weekends to finish the patio and deck, so we used every minute of the thin spring daylight. All except Bryan, who preferred to crawl from room to room in search of someone to play with. Home from the hospital not yet a year, he opened his eyes every morning with a look of surprise, happy for another day. We asked very little of him.

Oak trees in new leaf blew around me, shaking their
limbs. And I stood underneath what would become the deck,
helping my father nail crossbeams to one of the pillars. Given
a reprieve for the moment, Scott played with the pliers in
the shade of the cinderblock wall. My father's head was bent
in concentration as he pounded another nail into the wood,
while I tried to hold the boards straight.

"Hold it," my father said, "Don't let it slip. See, it's slipping."
He stopped his work and yanked the board back and forth
in my hands. "You have to hold it."

"I'm trying," I said.

"Try harder."

"I am," I whined.

"Get that tone out of your voice." He brought the hammer
up, ready to strike again.

"What tone?"

"That tone. Get it out of your voice and hold the boards."

I exhaled loudly and wagged the board before keeping
still; my hips canted to the side to indicate an impatience I
dared not voice. From the corner of my eye, I watched Scott
dig in the grass with the pliers. The whole project seemed
tedious and boring. No one had asked me if I wanted a deck.
We just all marched forward.

As my father pounded and muttered, I looked above me
to the unstained joists that were bolted to the pillars. What
I saw was not the sky, slanting through the frame my father
had built, but Bryan's tiny body. I blinked and looked again.

Bryan had crawled to the edge of the doorway on the
second floor of the house, the door that used to lead to a set
of stairs but now led to nothing. As he had been taught, he
had turned around and was prepared to scoot down backwards to reach what he thought was a stair.

I could see his feet combing the air for the next step. Fifteen feet below, we stood on the concrete. Only his arms kept him held to the doorsill.

"Dad!" I yelled. The hammering stopped. He looked at my hands for blood, sure he had somehow hit me or pinched my fingers between the boards.

"Bryan!" I yelled, pointing.

Bryan started to whimper and twist.

My father dropped his hammer. The boards I had been holding crashed to the ground. We both stared up, fixed on his white diaper and chubby legs.

"Go get him," he said.

"What!" I looked at him, sure I had heard wrong.

"I have to stay here in case he falls."

I envisioned my father waiting below my brother, arms wide, in hopes that when that tiny body fell he would have the agility and presence of mind to catch his son. I saw my father calculate the wind, the slant of sun, the rates at which he might fall.

"Worst-case scenario," my father said in my head. Imagine it and then proceed.

I pictured Bryan fallen at my feet. There would be blood, and splattering; and the white patio, so freshly laid it still shone in the sun, would be stained. My father adjusted his feet, moved slightly to the right, and held his hands to the sky.

I ran up the partially built stairs, carting the responsibility for my brother's life behind me. Did I think of the nail polish remover, the scars left on his throat from the acetone? Did I remember how his grafted skin turned shiny and blue in the cold? Did I stop for even a second and recognize that the responsibility was possibly not my own? Or did I simply run?

Balancing on the joists, I made my way to Bryan's side, not looking down at my father, at his lifted hands, squinting eyes. I told myself that I had to get there in time, that it was up to me, that I could not fail.

Scott had joined my father below, shading his eyes against the brightness. He didn't yell out, didn't say anything, just watched with his mouth open. In the distance, cars drove along busy Nutley Street. Perhaps my mother was in one of them, returning from the lumberyard, two-by-fours sticking out from the windows with red plastic flags stapled to the ends. She would pull into the driveway and notice the absence of hammerfalls, but what else?

I made it to the top of the deck frame, only feet from where Bryan dangled. Stepping on the boards, without looking down, I reached Bryan just as he stopped crying. His eyes were wide open, his small cheeks red with exertion. Mucous ran from his nose. I stood to the side of him, the slats of emptiness all around me, then bent closer to his frantic body. I grabbed his hands, pulled them from the edge of the doorsill. He let go immediately and released his weight, almost pulling both of us down. For a second I felt my balance shift, saw my father below me. It seemed certain we would fall. Then I sat back on the narrow beam, leveraged my brother's weight with my own and pulled him from the air. His naked body felt solid and certain in my lap. For once, he did not squirm. I heard more than saw my father make for the stairs to help us. We sat on a beam of redwood, my breath still coming fast, while the cars along Nutley continued on their way.

22

The Phone Call

The swimming pool turns out to have been a great decision.
Because of our time in Hawaii, Scott and I swim well. Every
day, we beg our mother to let us play in the pool. When she
first peels back the blue cover, the smell of chlorine burns
our noses.

One afternoon in the middle of summer, we are playing
with inflated inner tubes that we bought for a dollar from a
nearby gas station. Our bodies have already grown used to
the cold water, and our teeth no longer chatter. At one point,
my mother goes to the house and gets the chlorine test kit.
After she fills the tiny chambers, she holds the plastic vials
to the sun and calculates the strength.

Bryan plays on the deck nearby. Someone has given him
acorns to pile.

Above us the trees huddle in full-summer leaf. A circle
of blue, like the Catherine window in a cathedral, centers
directly over the pool. Every now and then a gray squirrel
leaps from one tree to the next, leaves shaking in his wake.
Other than that, the backyard is quiet. Even the traffic on
nearby Nutley Street seems to have halted on this cloying
afternoon.

"How many have you done?" I ask Scott, who is busy
hopping around in the pool collecting rubber tires.

"Three," he responds.

"I doubt it," I say. "I never saw three."

"Betcha." And he lunges for the last of four tires, before herding them like goats to the deck.

We are taking turns jumping through the hole in the pile of inner tubes. We stack one on top of the other and then leap from the pool deck. For the jump to "count," the stack cannot fall. Because the tires are inflated unevenly, each bulging in at least one place like blistered skin, they don't stack easily. Sometimes they topple before we have begun the countdown.

"Be careful," my mother says from the side of the pool where she is dumping the test vials back in. It's the distracted way in which she is always asking us to be careful, the same way she tells us to not play around doors. She must be planning dinner or considering paint colors against the walls of her mind.

I jump through the stack Scott has piled for me and hit the icy water. The rubber burns my upper arms where I miscalculated, and the stack falls. "You made them wobbly," I cry when I come to the surface. I can see the red welts forming already. They match the marks on my legs.

"The phone's ringing," my mother says. "I'll be right back."

I don't watch her walk the twenty yards to the house, past the beetle-infested roses, and climb the patio stairs, open the screen door, and enter the cool of the dining room. I am not there when she picks up the phone and greets Diane's mother who has called to complain about the construction at the Naval Yard.

Bryan remains on the pool deck. He throws each acorn to the ground below, pulls leaves from twigs. When it's my turn to jump through the tires, I stand only inches from where he sits on the wooden planks near my feet. I call Scott a cheater and threaten to stack my own tubes.

My mother remains in the house, perhaps wrapping the extra-long telephone cord around her body as she talks, every now and then trying to find a line of sight through the picture window to the pool. But she can't get the angle. She can't find her children. So she doesn't see the moment when Bryan topples into the pool. She doesn't see his arms flail, fingers grab at the blue plastic edge. She doesn't see him sink to the bottom, pulled by a diaper filled with water like a weight.

Nor do I.

He plummets, settles on the bottom, face up, blond hair waving like a water nymph's.

Having set my own stack of tires, balancing the blisters, fitting the rubber together like a puzzle, I climb the ladder to the deck and prepare for my jump. It is then that I see him, splayed like a frog against the bright blue bottom of the pool. His body shimmers under the water, the edges blurred, as if he has already begun to dissolve into the next world. This is how he sleeps, face up, arms thrown back, welcoming the night because he knows the worst thing he will ever face has already happened. Unlike me, who curls into a ball, blankets covering every inch of exposed flesh, afraid of the dark and monsters and being left alone.

He could be napping.

I don't yell to Scott. I don't say anything because I am consumed by the knowledge that I was the one left in charge, and I can't dive four feet to pull his body from the water. Even if I could bring him to the surface, I don't know how to save him. The fallen tires bump against the edges of the pool, leaves gather on the surface.

I begin to scream.

23

The Video

One evening at Hospital Point, in the weeks before the movers would come to pack us out and take our household goods across the Pacific to Virginia, my father suggested we watch home movies. The dishes were done, laundry folded, the items on my mother's invisible list crossed off for the day.

"It'll be fun," my father said, already headed for the closet that held the film projector.

My mom sat on the couch, her feet tucked beneath her, her needlepoint tipped toward the lamp for better light. Scott, almost three, played with his trucks on the floor. I watched my mother pull the purple thread through the canvas. A few days earlier I had asked what she was making with all those shades of purple. A sampler, she had told me, and I nodded, though I had no clearer picture of what the needlepoint would become.

I did know that once the sampler was finished another project would take its place, hemming my skirt, patching Scott's pants, ironing the stiff creases into my father's uniform. My mother's hands never stilled. I imagined even in sleep they kept moving, perhaps refiguring the checkbook that always left her frustrated or kneading another loaf of bread. If we did watch a home movie that night, my mother would see very little of it.

My father set the projector on the dining room table and told me to find pillows for the floor. The military-white walls made a sheet unnecessary. It also meant that geckos and the occasional cockroach would make guest appearances on screen.

"WHAT SHOULD WE watch?" my father asked. He turned toward my mother, but I was the one who responded.

"My birthday, my birthday," I cried, abandoning the shadow puppets on the wall and hurrying to his side.

The breeze from the harbor filled our tiny living room, vibrating the Venetian blinds. Most of the movies were from my father's childhood, grainy films of boys chasing one another around picnic tables piled high with Tupperware or movies from dinner parties where guest after guest held half-full glasses to the camera and cheered the lens.

My father glanced at my mother, who merely shrugged her shoulders mid-stitch.

"Your birthday it is," he said.

The bright square of white was replaced by the scratch and blur of film being loaded. I sprawled on the floor, my head on a cushion, and listened to the click of the projector as it moved the film forward. Nothing, black scratches, white light, then nothing, then thread-like lines, then black, then nothing, then my one-year-old self, sitting in a high chair, pig tails sprouting like fireworks from both sides of my head.

"There I am," I cried, though I felt no sense of recognition or connection between the girl on the screen before me and the one I understood myself to be. I couldn't have said for sure it was my mother, the woman who hovered near my highchair, hair piled in some kind of crazy bouffant with a white headband holding it all back. The woman wore pearls, like my mother sometimes did, but the woman on film smiled more freely. Or maybe she didn't smile more, but rather when she did smile it seemed like the natural resting expression for her face, the pauses between smiles becoming the oddity. I looked over at my mother now, craning her body toward the light in the even darker room my father had insisted on for the movie.

"Damnit," my mother said softly, putting her finger to her mouth to suck. Then she resumed her needlework, and I imagined a drop of blood on the deep purple thread, woven into the sampler, known only to the two of us.

"There you are!" my father cried. "And look at you! Look at what you're doing with that cake!"

What I was doing was repairing my cake. Chocolate cake, one my mother had made, with two even layers, and frosting that shone even on film. I had taken the first bite, maybe the first two, or five, or ten, and then, noticing the holes made by my greedy hands, I had gone about repairing the damage, mushing the cake crumbs back to the cake, smoothing over the frosting.

"What a girl!" my father said, his bourbon refilled, the ice clinking in the glass.

The damaged cake magically repaired under my one-year-old hands and in front of my five-year-old eyes, so that by the end I was sitting above a perfectly formed cake, clapping my hands, the candles now relit.

When the film finished, I asked to see it again, delighting in my ability to fix the cake, my intelligence, my cleverness. And for once my father didn't argue, didn't criticize, didn't ration joy like flour. He played it again and then again, so that when we had finished, the night was certain and dark, stars bright above the inky black harbor.

Only recently did I learn that my father had been playing the film backwards, a fact that seems as obvious now as it was magical then. Again and again my father would wind the film and hit reverse. The story of a girl who lived her life carefully, a lie. I had eaten my cake with the abandon of every other one-year-old.

Somewhere inside me lives the girl who couldn't stand to see the ugliness of a mess, the insides of her cake exposed and crumbling. A daughter of the military, she believes order and regulation will defeat evil and disarray. She will never leave crumbs on the counter and will always turn off the lights.

24

The Mask

My mother stands on the deck with Bryan in her hands. All around us the crows caterwaul in the trees, competing with the traffic to see who can fill the air with sound. Down the street a lawn mower comes on and then cuts off almost immediately. I hear a semi braking at the stoplight, gears downshifting and the squeal of hot brakes.

My mother doesn't hold Bryan to her chest but rather to the sky, offering her son to the crows, the clouds, the errant leaf. Water rushes from her t-shirt, my brother's diaper, his hair; it streams in channels that pour through the boards of the deck, hitting the hard red clay, and spattering the white sides of the pool with red. Still holding him to the sky, she screams, something fierce and deep, a sound that renders every other sound ever made a whisper.

"Oh God," she sobs. "Oh my God, no! No, no, no!"

Offering his body on an altar of air, she calls again and again to the clouds, while the trees all around us hold the scene like a globe, a world that's been shaken.

MY MOTHER LEARNED to SCUBA dive in Hawaii, is trained in CPR, first aid, the specific strategies you employ to save someone whose lungs have filled with water. But she does not press his chest or clear his throat, does not put her mouth to his. Confused, I stand by the pile of red dirt, caught in a world that no longer makes sense, where brothers drown and mothers wail and daughters forget to watch.

"I'll call Dad," I shout.

Instead of answering me, she bends over my brother, still unable to put him down. Forming a half bench on her knees, she begins to press his chest.

I think of my father, miles away, deep in the belly of the Pentagon, shuffling papers and talking to his secretary, unaware of what is unfolding in his own backyard. He should know what is happening. He could do something. He knows how to fix everything, has every tool possible hanging from the pegboard in his workshop.

"I'll call Dad," I yell again.

And this time she hears me because she turns toward me and looks surprised to see that she is not alone in this hell.

"Go to the Walters! Call 911!"

"No, Dad," I say, heading to the house. He is the only one who can make this okay.

"The Walters! Call 911!"

Only much later will I realize that I am too young to call the ambulance on my own. I have let my brother drown, but I can't reach the kitchen phone without the heavy stool. The wind picks up and carries away the possibility of my father saving us. I run to the neighbors, leaving my mother holding my brother limp in her arms.

Through sheer force of will, my mother will suck the chlorinated water from Bryan's lungs and keep him in this world. The ambulance will be returned to the hospital, and my mother will keep Bryan close. When he sleeps in her arms, he will look exactly as he did under water, face soft, edges blurred, eyelashes still and quiet.

And here is what gives me pause all these many years later: we will wait for my father to come home, wait to hear his heels hit the stone pathway, to tell him. In doing so, it will be clear to me that this day, this event, this moment, is not exceptional. It didn't even warrant a phone call. We will keep all of this—the wailing, the water, the boy blurring into the next world—under control.

"I'm home," my father calls, as he opens the front door. Scott and I sit in the living room, under strict orders not to utter a word. My mother holds Bryan at the dining room table, place settings tidy, water glasses already filled. Perhaps she has not called him because she wants to share the story with the evidence of a good ending in her arms.

"Hey guys," my father says when he moves past the bamboo screen and sees us on the living room floor. "I bought you something."

He holds a plain brown bag in his hands, the kind from the military exchange, and offers it to us.

"Thanks, Dad," we chorus, glancing toward my mother. Is it okay to take a present on a day your younger brother almost dies?

"There are two, so you can each have one. No fighting over colors."

He moves toward the stairs, already unbuttoning his uniform. "How was your day?" he asks my mom.

Inside the brown paper bag are two masks and snorkels, one blue and one red. Even at that age, I understand the irony as I place the mask against my face and imagine an underwater world.

In the kitchen, my parents draw close to the sink under the only window in the room, and my mother tells my father how his son almost died that day. I am sure she takes the blame for all of it, has no idea that I am already carrying my own suitcase of guilt. I imagine my father holds both my mother and brother closely, says comforting words, but he will never fully understand. He has never heard my mother scream so loudly that the crows are sent flying. He has never seen his son blur at the edges. Perhaps she skips the part about pleading with the sky or the way Bryan's body was made heavy by the diaper even though all the life had drained from him. Maybe she doesn't show him the deep scrape in her side where she brushed against the boards on the deck as she ran to her son. I don't know what they say to each other. Their murmurs lap into the living room and collect in the lamplight where they surround Scott and me who hold new masks in our hands. Outside in the long summer evening, birds return to their nests and the sky begins to quiet down.

25

The Cereal

In her thirties, The Dead Baby will study trauma. Ordinary trauma. She will write about military children whose boots never touch the ground but who instead ride the backs of deactivated missiles while their parents meet and greet at the base chapel, who stand on the shore and wave to their fathers who line the decks of destroyers in orange life preservers, who sit in the backseat of the station wagon as it weaves between antiterrorist barricades in order to get home. For them, no division exists between a battlefield and a bedroom. Every day their fathers prepare for war. This reality is their ordinary and made to appear ordinary by the same military that transforms individuals into corp.

Though she won't write about it then, The Dead Baby remembers the bugle, notes swimming through the air. She remembers her mother pulling to the side of the road with the other vehicles, uniformed soldiers standing at attention, knuckle to brow, and the mournful sound of Taps rolling through the car. How every single person on the base, including her, turned toward a flag none could see but all saluted.

THE ORDINARY PASSES unnoticed. It is all we do not see in our days. Were we to remark on an event—the Marine with the gun at the gate who salutes our car—then it would no longer be ordinary. The ordinary leaves no mark, creates no stories.

The military child ingests mutually assured destruction with her breakfast cereal. They appear the same.

How, The Dead Baby wonders in her thirties, might you document moments that pass unnoticed—that were made to pass unnoticed—but that undid you nevertheless? It couldn't be a story with a beginning, middle, and end. That would be too tidy and too certain. In fact, she thinks, it couldn't be a story at all. The Dead Baby knows that even now, as an adult, she keeps moving boxes and packing paper in the closet under the stairs. She remains in so many ways the girl she was. And she knows The Dead Baby did not arrive at the age of eight able to articulate why she counted pennies. She didn't understand at sixteen that the shame she experienced around her body had roots in the enlisted men she stood in line behind at the Navy Exchange with naked women tattooed on their forearms. Nor could she have connected her inadequacy to the stories her father told of his childhood spent on a farm where violence was as common as corn.

It is only decades after her service has ended that she can start to put these things together, place them side by side, begin to fathom how the past is never past, anger is not the absence of love, and buckets come with handles for carrying.

26

The Fall

For years, my father has gotten up before daylight and immersed himself in war—how to prevent one, how to win one, how to make it legal, tidy, and clean. It is my mother who greets me when I return from school, my mother who ferries me to the dentist, to Girl Scouts, the one who French braids my hair. While Bryan almost drowns in the backyard pool my father built, the one he filled with water from a garden hose, my father is reading confidential files on the Middle East, a cup of tepid coffee resting inches from his fingertips. At seven, I can't forgive my father for leaving me to face my mother's naked suffering on my own.

For the length of the school year we avoid any more ambulances, and I pull lengths of moss from between the tree roots and make beds for my stuffed animals. Our second, and final, summer in Virginia we return, cautiously, to the pool. Sometimes I stand on the deck and look at the plastic liner on the bottom, imagining my brother, nymph-like, below.

Toward the end of June, in the summer of 1976, when I am seven, Scott is five, and Bryan not yet two, my parents leave the three of us with a babysitter for the evening. We eat TV dinners and watch television. The babysitter talks on the phone. My parents rarely go out—too expensive—so the sitter is a special treat. We are disappointed, though, that she doesn't get down on the floor and play with us, and soon we grow bored.

At some point, Scott and I climb onto the top of the couch and wrestle each other on the narrow edge. The babysitter ignores us: Dynasty is on. Outside, the darkness settles against the house, the last light from the summer sun long gone. Scott pushes me off the back and I fall onto the cushions. Next time, I push him.

And then I am falling and never land. One minute I am standing on the back of the couch, the lava not yet returned, wrestling with Scott while the babysitter watches television, and the next, I am sitting on the wicker table, as the baby-sitter and her mother, a thick woman smelling of oregano, ice my head and insist that I am okay. Upon regaining consciousness, I can only think that I should not be on the table, a washcloth filled with ice leaking water down the back of my neck.

That I never land breaks the narrative of my life neatly in two, leaving a narrow crevasse. No one is ever sure how long I remained unconscious on the floor. The babysitter keeps changing her story and Scott only says, "ten thousand minutes."

The babysitter lies to my parents, or more literally, fails to mention the part where I lie unconscious—for seconds, minutes, forever—on the carpet-covered concrete slab of the basement floor, thereby dismantling the only possible bridge between the seven-year-old I was and the seven-year-old I have become. The gap is a secret, one I am willing to keep. I should not have been on the back of the couch. I should not have been fighting with my brother. My parents are standing over me, talking in whispers, feeling the bump on the back of my head. A "goose egg," they call it, pressing their fingers into hair tangled and matted with blood. The light is on, but I feign sleep in hopes my father will carry me from my parents' bed to my own. He does, holding me close enough that I can smell the pungent mix of food and alcohol remaining on his breath.

When I awake the next morning, the world itself has split. I see two of everything: two doors, two beds, two mothers, two heads. This, too, I keep secret.

I suffer from a subdermal hematoma, a swelling of blood against the brain, common after severe head trauma. Specifically, the blood is pushing on the optic nerve, causing my eyes to cross like Wyle E. Coyote's after he has been smashed by a giant boulder. For days I live in a twinned reality, unable to fuse the image and its double. Watching the world multiply, intrigued by my inability to grasp a glass or a book, dizzy from walking up or down stairs, I imagine I'm a magician, that I can heal or walk on water, fly through the air. Mostly, though, I am scared.

My mother finally takes me to the doctor when she and my father notice my difficulty walking. I sit on an orange plastic chair just outside the doctor's office while my mother calls the Pentagon to let my father know what is happening.

"I have to admit her right now," she says. Then a pause.

"Bethesda," she clarifies. I imagine a long silence on both ends of the phone. The place where Bryan was burned.

I realize she means the hospital and that "now" means right now. I won't be going home for dinner. Sitting in a chair where my feet can't touch the ground, I close my eyes to shut out the multiplication of that reality.

If I spoke with my father that afternoon, I have no recollection of the conversation. My guess is my parents were consumed with the details of childcare, carpools, and the need to make dinner for my brothers. It feels as though I do not see or talk to my father for several days. He orbits our family, an outer planet, dark and far away. I rarely see him in daylight, except with a wrench in his hand bent over a toilet or car engine fixing what has fallen apart. At those moments he finds it unfathomable that I cannot shine the flashlight where he needs it.

27

The Sun

In the hospital bed next to mine rests a girl, a few years older, in a full body cast, head to foot. The doctors have cut a perfectly round circle in the plaster at her belly, like a hole in a sheet of ice, a place for her skin to breathe. For entire afternoons the girl's mother rubs her daughter's stomach, drawing her fingers in increasingly smaller circles, following an invisible vortex to the center. The girl in the cast cannot turn her head to look at me, but I know she knows I watch her. The nurses bring her meals that she can drink through a very long straw. I leave my food untouched.

"What a pretty day," my mother says, when she comes to visit on one of the first afternoons. Through a series of windows, sunlight slants into the yellow-painted room, but the windows are cruelly high. I have to trust the day is fine based on the beams of light I see.

Exhausted from seeing double, I sleep most of the time or watch my dual mothers hover. They usually come in the mornings, after Scott goes to school and Bryan is dropped at daycare.

"It's so warm out there, Jennifer, you wouldn't believe it. The roses were wilting before I left."

She glances over to the girl in the cast. "Hi," she says brightly enough, though strained. Her eyes keep returning to the girl for long moments, while she begins to unpack the bag of books she has brought, then rearranges them on the shelf nearby. I cannot tell if she is relieved my body is not broken or if she wishes my injury could be healed as easily as setting a bone.

"How do you feel?" she asks, returning to me. Her fingers tickle my forehead, then my cheeks, then she pops up and fiddles with the books again.

Sometimes while my mother is with me, I wiggle my toes and run my hands back and forth under the stiff white sheet, moving to make up for the girl who is as still as death. Other times I wrap the sheet tight around my legs and imagine what it feels like to be encased in plaster. I keep my head facing forward and only move my eyes. After a few minutes of this, though, I unwind the sheet.

No one signs my roommate's cast; it remains blank like a beach after the tide.

At night, long after my mother has left and the nurses' station is quiet, I cry in the darkness. Having overheard the doctor say that the very worst thing you can do after a severe head injury is to allow the person to sleep, I am scared to drift off. I worry that I will not wake up, that I am still in danger, that I will end once again, while the girl in the cast learns to walk, her body bound by plaster no longer and her skin tingling at the touch of the sun or cotton or the bubbles in her bath, and my brothers become old enough to visit the children's ward in the hospital, although there will no longer be reason to, and my parents grieve for the death of their daughter but eventually return to tending the garden, picking up the groceries, and reading the morning paper, while the babysitter spends her days working in a tiny booth in a parking garage and wondering how Alexis will ever work things out on *Dynasty*.

My mother presses the sheet around me, tucks the thin cotton blanket under my sides. "Keep warm," she says.

I nod at both mothers.

"Next time I'll have to remember my jacket. I have forgotten how cold hospitals always are. You wouldn't know it was so hot outside."

She glances at the girl, then back to me, tucks the blanket even tighter, like a coat of armor, though I'm not sure what I'm being protected from.

"I remember when your grandmother was in the hospital. I froze to death. Finally had to go to the mall and buy a sweater. I don't know why they keep it like this. Maybe to freeze the germs."

She shivers and wraps her arms around her body.

"You can have my blanket," I say, my eyes now closed, drifting back to sleep where I see just one of everything.

"No," she says. "No, you need that."

I don't have to open my eyes to know she is looking at the girl in the cast.

One thing I learn very quickly in the hospital is the many ways a body can break. On the night after I meet a blind girl during art therapy class, I fall asleep grateful that I can see two of everything rather than nothing at all.

28

The Needle

The needle seems as long as my thigh, and I only catch sight of it when the nurse picks it up from the metal tray and hands it over my curled and naked body to the doctor. My mother stands next to me on the examination table, bright lights bouncing off the metal surfaces. She arrived minutes before the spinal tap.

"You have to lie perfectly still," the doctor says.

I nod as best I can, my head pressed tight to the white paper that covers the examination table.

"I mean totally still, like you're dead. Do you understand?"

I nod again.

"If you move, you'll be paralyzed."

The examination room is cold; I shiver. The drape they have given me is thin and covers only the front of my body. The doctor runs his finger along my spine. It bumps over each vertebra.

"Do you think she can remain still?" he asks my mother. "We can restrain her." I see the nurse hold up thick bands with buckles that jangle in the chilly air.

My mother stands in front of my curled body, has seen the needle, heard the risks. She rubs my forehead with her fingers, a soft, even rhythm like the surf. "She'll be fine," she says. Then turning to me, in my ear, "Won't you."

Immediately the desire to move consumes me. Itches are everywhere, tickles and twitches, limbs falling asleep and begging to be stirred.

I think of working around my father's power tools, being told that one wrong move on my part will leave him fingerless or dead. While my dad soldered, welded, or sawed, I imagined what would happen if I failed to hold the boards the way they needed to be held or let the two wires touch— a slip of the saw meant red blood fountaining from a fingerless hand and my father screaming in pain while I tried to locate the missing digits amid the inch-thick layer of sawdust that covered the garage floor.

Lying on the doctor's table, fighting the urge to move and knowing I will fail once the needle goes in, I contemplate remaining in this fetal position for life, like the girl in the cast. Tracing his hand along my spine, the doctor tells me he is about to insert the needle.

"Look at me," my mother says, the softness replaced with steel. "Look at me."

Her face hovers near mine, her blue eyes strong and forceful.

"Count tea kettles with me, starting with one. Don't think of what's happening."

Tears start to come, though the doctor is just feeling my spine.

"Control your mind, Jennifer. Count with me. Now."

And we start to count kettles of tea.

"One steam kettle, two steam kettles, three steam kettles," we intone together.

Her eyes never leave mine, even when I break from her stare to look toward my stomach where I expect the head of the needle to emerge from my backside.

We are on the fifteenth teakettle when the needle goes in. My mother's eyes pin me to the table, willing me to remain still.

29

The Test

After the first few days in the hospital, my mother senses that I am improving, even though all the tests indicate no such thing. Or maybe she wants to will it so. When she arrives in the mornings, she brings a book filled with project ideas as well as supplies. The key to healing, my mother implies by the sheer weight of her crafts bag, lies in keeping mind and hands engaged. Sitting in bed, in new pink pajamas with tiny flowers that vine around the neck, I wind God's eyes out of yarn scraps and glue Popsicle stick furniture while she tells me stories about my brothers and reads the get well cards sent by my relatives. The girl in the cast has been moved to another room or has been released. No one tells me which. There are several empty beds, so we have plenty of space to work. My God's eyes come out crooked again and again, the crossed pieces far from perpendicular. I cannot tell if it is my vision or my hands that cause them to bend and turn, but the result suggests that God's eyes are as warped as my own. My mother tapes them to the wall beside my bed, and I am surrounded with bent vision.

The doctors are puzzled by the failure of my head to heal. While the bump is no longer hard—it has grown soft and mushy—it has not disappeared. I finger it when no one is looking, pushing the blood from one end to the other, playing with the waterbed of skin.

Late one afternoon the doctor takes my mother into the hall. They whisper outside my door, but I can hear.

"It's an old test," he says. "To be honest, we're not really sure why it works. But it can give us more information."

"I thought the thing you did yesterday was this great new test. I thought that was going to tell you everything."

The day before I had been one of the first people in the country to undergo a CAT scan. Doctors and nurses stood, several rows thick, around the giant machine, while they rolled my body into a metal cave and told me to remain, once again, perfectly still. It felt like a circus but without the popcorn. Several people actually clapped when they rolled me back out again.

The test the doctor wants to do now sounds much more terrifying.

"You really have to hang her upside down?"

"Yes, but not for long."

"How long?"

"Until she throws up."

I hear the custodian pushing the mop bucket down the hall, a nearby buzzer going off, the soft snore of the girl who sleeps on the far side of my room now. I wait for my mother to rise and say no, to refuse such a terrible test. I wait to hear the edge in her voice that tells me she has drawn the line, and here is where it is.

"If the blood is not reabsorbed over the next twenty-four hours, we'll have no choice but to try this," the doctor says.

She sighs. "Okay."

That night I push the mushy bump into my skull, hoping to convince the blood to go back to where it came from. In

the morning I measure my success, but the bump remains.
I practice for the test by leaning my head over the hospital
bed, examining the springs on the underside, the mattress
tag, waiting for the nausea. Within seconds, the pressure
increases in my neck and ears and feels as though I am
trapped beneath a wave. I stop practicing.

The day of the test arrives, but my mother does not. I am
pushed down the halls in a wheelchair by an orderly who
appears unconcerned about the test that awaits me.

"Where's my mother?" I ask.

"No idea," the man says, then calls over to a passing nurse,
"Hey, pretty lady."

"My mother has to be here."

"Sweetheart, I'm just the driver. I drive them where they
need to go. I don't know anything about your mother."

I start to cry.

"Hey, pretty lady," he calls to another nurse, just as he turns
me into a waiting room full of empty chairs but no mother.

The walls of the waiting room are bare except for a few
framed pictures of naval ships and a map depicting the emergency routes. I think about what it will feel like to hang
upside down until I throw up. Will they bind my ankles with
straps? Dangle me with others from the ceiling?

At the ages of five and six, my dad would pick me up from
my ankles and swing me around like the blade of a helicopter.
Around and around he would spin me, my head only inches
from the ground, all the time laughing. Trees and bushes, the
legs of those nearby, would fly past, blurring into a stream
of color. My weight balanced against his; I could feel him
relying on my body to keep his upright. The faster we spun,
the more we mattered to one another in terms of our balance. Faster and faster, my head thick with blood and force.

Or was I crying? My ankles burned where his hands held me, a fire where we touched. Sometimes he bumped me on the ground, my nose, my forehead, dirt and grass. The helicopter would slow down, the world coming back into focus, and I would feel, at first, relief. The blood would leave my face, the heaviness, and the sting would subside from my ankles, even though I could see his fingers, lines of red, etched into my skin. He would move onto the next child, a brother, a friend.

"More, more," I would cry, tears on my cheeks, my heart still pounding. "Again!" Because even though it hurt, and even though I was scared, for those few moments, I had my father to myself, locked together by centrifugal force. Maybe the test worked in the same way: a kind of damage in exchange for possibility. I accepted those terms all the time.

The same orderly who had delivered me not ten minutes before appears at the door with an empty wheelchair. Dog tags rattle under his army-green smock.

"Your test is cancelled, sweetheart. I'm here to drive you back to your room."

30

The Cookies

The possibility of connection with my father comes the very next day, as if one test was exchanged for another. But when he appears in my room, rapping on the doorframe, dressed in cotton pants and a button-down shirt, I don't feel delight, only anger. That morning on the phone my mother told me the blood had started to subside, and I would be going home soon. My vision was returning to normal. She had promised to bring the yellow yarn octopus we had been making for the past few afternoons, days in which I had my mother all to myself, days without kitchens to clean and laundry to fold and diapers to change. I had expected to see her and her giant bag of crafts. I had been listening for her voice calling the nurses by name as she passed their station, remarking on the weather or the traffic or how late she was.

My father had only visited a few other times and never by himself. His long work hours meant he couldn't spend whole mornings with me, and when he was home at night he took care of my brothers so that my mom could visit me, turning lemon-yellow yarn into octopus arms. Today, ten days into my hospital stay, he arrives alone.

We are both awkward. My father doesn't know the protocol, where to sit, what to do when the nurses come in to take my temperature, whether or not I am allowed to leave my bed. And he has brought no projects, no bag of crafts, not even a game.

I am angry that he does not know how to act. Angry that he has come in place of, into the place of, my mother who rubs my face and reads books to me while the afternoon sun sinks down the walls of the hospital room. I am angry that he does not notice the girl in the cast has somehow left before me, even though she cannot walk.

"Where's Mom?" I ask before he even has time to say hello. I peer around his outstretched hands, listening for her laughter in the hall. But she is not there.

"She's home with your brothers. I came to see you today instead. Maybe we can go for a walk." He looks around for a door to the outside lawn, a path, a place to walk.

"Why didn't Mom come with you?"

"She's at home today. We thought it would be nice if I got to spend time with you. I brought you some cookies."

He has stopped by the vending machines down the hallway and brought me a package of Fig Newtons. He understands nothing. Fig Newtons are carrot sticks. They are no treat.

"What have you been up to today?"

He tries to sit on the bed, but I don't move my legs. Instead he perches on the edge for a moment and, unable to find enough space, stands up again. It is not readily apparent where he can put his hands, so he crosses them against his chest and smiles at me.

"Have you had lunch?" he asks, looking around the room for a tray. Out of his uniform, he seems a little less tall, a little less certain, or maybe his hesitation has less to do with what he's wearing and more to do with the situation. It is unusual to see him in anything other than a uniform or the clothes he wears to build garages, decks, patios, and the toys he makes for my brothers and me late at night, long after I am asleep. Sawdust does not cling to his pants. His hands, always covered in cuts and scrapes, finally move to his pockets.

"I want Mom."

"She's not here." We both look around the room and ascertain that she is, indeed, not here. He glances at the God's eyes taped to the wall, bends to touch one. It wobbles and falls to the bed. He moves back.

"I want Mom," I say again, louder. I hear the desperation in my voice. I don't know how to act with my dad, what to do. I grip my pillow, think about throwing it, but where? To the floor? To the wall? Instead, I kick my covers and the fallen God's eye hits the floor.

"What do you and Mom do? We could do that."

"I want Mom!" I know I am yelling because I hear the soft but solid footsteps of the nurses as they leave their station and move down the hall toward my room.

We do not go for a walk. I have turned towards the wall of crooked eyes and do not see the expression on his face when he says goodbye. The Fig Newtons remain on the table next to my bed until the evening nurse comes by and throws them away.

A few days later, I am released from the hospital, just in time for Independence Day 1976. We go to D.C. to watch the parade, marching band after marching band, so many flags. No one talks about the hospital. I never apologize to my father. The yellow yarn octopus, though, remains on my bed. At least for a week. After that, the movers come and pack our boxes. Days later, we are gone.

31

The Rock

The movers don't pack the lava. Sometime while I am in the hospital, my mother places the rock in a box without a return address and sends it back to Hawaii Volcano National Park. This piece joins thousands returned that year.

My parents never mention the lava or the curse. They never tell me Pele has been appeased. They never say anything to suggest that a burned newborn, a near drowning, and a concussed daughter in the space of two years is anything out of the ordinary. But I am unable to cope. I have seen the inside of my head, have seen the world halved, and watched my mother blow life into my brother's dripping body. I have no lava to return. And there are not enough pennies in the can.

32

The Cave

Instead, in the spring of second grade, I simply stopped going to school.

One day I raised my hand in class to say that I wasn't feeling well and within the hour my mother had come and taken me home. Good girls, I quickly learned, could lie to great effect. Only utter a few words, and I was excused to the cool, dark cave of the nurse's office and almost as easily transported home. My mother was but a few words away.

I loved to lie in that room waiting for my mother to come. Down a short hallway but still within the main office, the sick room hovered perfectly between solitude and communion. Alone on the bed in a cinderblock room that reminded me of our basement at home, I would listen to the chatter of the secretaries in the office, answering the phones, making announcements on the PA system, shuffling papers, and collecting attendance. Accompanied by the purpled fumes of freshly mimeographed pages, the quiet hum of the office was familiar in its daily replication.

The first time my mother appeared, it was as if by magic. My simple words had summoned her back to me. And in that moment, having been guided gently on the shoulder by the nurse and brought into the light of the main office and to my mother, I learned that language could cast a spell.

The distance between home and school could be traveled. I only had to hold my stomach and cry.

So the next day I raised my hand again. And again, I was sent to the nurse's office to lie on the bed and again my mother appeared, shaking her head in concern, carrying Bryan in her arms. At home, she put me to bed and left me to rest. My temperature sat at 98.6. I had no cough, no runny nose. When pushed, I complained of a stomachache. Safe in my room, I listened to the muffled household sounds, the kitchen faucet turning on and off, my father calling home, pots and pans being shuffled in the preparation for dinner.

THE FIRST FEW days I spent in the nurse's office waiting for my mother, I felt special. The kind nurse shook her head and said, "Poor baby." Her hand on my cheek, we waited for the thermometer. Before turning out the light, she would find me a second blanket in case I got cold.

My mother was no different. Usually intolerant of illness, convinced that sickness lived only in your head, those first few days I came home from school my mother hovered. From the safety of my bed, I listened to the sounds of her day. Every now and then she would poke her head into my room. "Need anything?" Perhaps she thought the difficulties of the past two years justified some extra time in bed. Each morning, though, she would send me to school again, sure that both my mind and body were recovered.

By the fourth day, people were on to me. The teacher questioned me when I raised my hand. "Are you going to be sick to your stomach? Can you wait until the end of reading period? Can you wait until the end of the day?" Firm in my resolve and fearful at the apparent failure of my words, I begged to go and see the nurse. The teacher allowed me to leave but more begging was required once I got to the main office. In fact, by the end of the week, I was having to throw a fit, just to be allowed entrance into the darkened room. For hours, for the entire length of the school day, no one checked on me. They knew I did not have a fever. No one called my mother. She did not appear. Behind the now-closed door, I could hear no office noises, no quiet hum, no surf. I lay on the bed in darkness.

When my mother finally appeared at the end of the day, her face was drawn in anger, not concern. She took me to the doctor. He poked and prodded, listened and tested, and returned me to my mother with a clean bill of health. There was nothing wrong with me, this quiet girl who never spoke in class, who never interrupted, who never caused a ruckus and always took the cookie that was closest to her when offered. She was fine.

The next day my mother drove me to school.

"You need to stay at school. I don't want them calling me."

"Okay," I said.

"I'm not coming to get you. Do you understand?" Her eyes left the road and looked at me.

I said nothing, watched the northern Virginia trees whip by my window.

"Has anything happened? Do you want to tell me anything?"

Another girl, an older one maybe, could explain the panic that seized her when she boarded the school bus in the morning, could connect the physical separation from her mother each morning to other moments in her life when she was left alone. But there was no one else in the car. She looked behind her seat just to make sure.

"It's okay, Mom."

The car took a corner and my backpack slid from the seat to the floor; I determined I would never go to the nurse's den again.

A FEW WEEKS before my illness, my grandpa and grandma babysat me and my brothers while my parents went to the Bahamas. I remember my grandpa teaching me how to cheat at solitaire. I also remember standing at the picture window, a deck of cards in one hand, on the day my parents were to return. I don't, however, remember what he did at night when everyone was supposed to be sleeping. Nor do I remember the name he called me when he came into my room. Perhaps it never happened.

You would like to think you can trust that blank space in your life, that week when your grandparents took care of you, but you worry the one protecting you is Memory itself, granting you a necessary emptiness. Memory works that way. You have felt her slip beneath you before. Remember that banyan tree, the one that dropped its roots like a woman might her hair not far from the demolished hospital on Hospital Point? Remember how you ran along the burned out foundation, kiawe scrub pushing through the cracks in the cement? That hospital wasn't there. Or, more to the point, it was. Your mother told you years later when you shared your memory of the building's collapse that the hospital remained, empty but intact, floors and floors, linoleum, porcelain sinks. You and Scott ran the wide halls and listened to the echo of your voices. Your shrieks might still remain lodged in the ceiling panels along with dust and tropical air.

But you remember devastation instead.

You remember a hospital leveled to its foundation with a five-year-old's hope that the bombs had already dropped.

And when your parents leave you alone with your grand-parents for the week, Memory pulls the covers up, tucks you into bed.

33

The Tractor

I finish second grade. Our household goods, minus the lava, are shipped across the country, and we are relocated to Washington State so my father can complete a Master's degree in maritime law. To save money, we drive our beat-up Ford from Virginia to Seattle, perhaps lapping the moving van that holds our furniture, perhaps meeting the military family that is renting our house from us, the child who will occupy my room, swim in the pool, walk down the hill in the foggy fall mornings. We drive from Virginia to Nebraska without stop, straight through the night. Thirty-six hours. No need for a motel room. To keep awake, my father stuffs tobacco between his cheek and gum and rolls down the window for fresh air. My brothers and I sleep sitting up in the backseat. Every few hours, I open my eyes and see my father peering into the darkness. Sometimes he is singing to himself. Other times he is jiggling his thighs, slapping his forearms to stay alert.

In Cozad, Nebraska, my father's childhood home, we stop. My brothers and I wake the minute the car leaves the inter-state, so I see when we turn into my grandparents' driveway. Even though it is late in the evening, the colors from the sunset still rinse the sky. The two lakes—one in the front and one on the side of their ranch house—glow orange. With the car windows up and the air conditioner on, I can still hear the crickets chirring.

We pass my grandparents' wishing well where Little Black Sambo and his sister fish off the edge; the gravel driveway announces our arrival. While it has only been a year since our last visit, aunts and uncles stand in front of the garage, cups of coffee in hand, waiting to greet the only brother who ever really left. Light spills from the kitchen window, illuminating everyone but my grandpa. He stands in the shadow of the garage, taking his time. Even though I can barely see him, I know what he is wearing: loose polyester pants, an olive button-down shirt, and burgundy-red suspenders holding his bones and skin together.

MY GRANDPARENTS' HOUSE sits astride two lakes, ovals of mossy green water that warm in the summer like a bathtub and are populated by sunfish, perch, and blue gill. They call their place "Twin Lakes Villa," but the lakes are far from identical. The moss in one grows so thick that swimming proves impossible, while the second, the one in front of their house, runs smaller and deeper, the place I spend long summer days. Now eight, I am allowed to swim in the lake unsupervised. My cousins and I navigate the paddleboat to the middle of the lake and jump from the silver pontoons. Pat, my grandparents' flea-bitten dog, sometimes swims halfway out to meet us but usually tires quickly and returns to the shore, leaving ripples in his wake.

Other times we play Barbies in the spare room, opening the Barbie airplane that my Aunt Brenda played with when she was a girl. We bend the dolls' legs so they can sit at the tiny table or strap them into the seat reserved for the flight attendant. Two blonde men pilot the Barbie plane, their figures painted onto the plastic. One has blue eyes and looks at us, a hand raised in a wave, ready to wink.

The closet in the spare room is full of toys that Brenda once played with. The only girl in a family of four boys, she had been so wanted. By the time she arrived in the early fifties, my grandpa had left farming and was doing well in real estate. The fact that her Barbies spill from the closet when we slide open the door shows how much her parents loved her. All afternoon, we sit on the floor of the spare room, a rug hanging like a tapestry on the wall depicting a hunting scene, two rifles not six feet above our heads resting in a wooden gun holder, and a black-and-white checked hide-a-bed that the three of us sleep in at night.

A few days into our visit, my grandpa asks me to mow the lawn with him, a chore he usually leaves for others, but decides on this day to take care of himself. He owns a large green riding lawn mower, a small tractor really, with a black vinyl seat and a grass catcher mounted on the back. When I climb up to sit with him in the driving seat, my grandpa opens his legs and motions to the space between them. He is wearing long pants even though the day is already hot.

By midsummer in central Nebraska, evenings fail to cool, and the early morning heat materializes in a thick haze that clutches and holds the land. I look forward to the moments when my grandpa steers the tractor into the shade of trees, coolness rippling up my legs. Such moments are scarce, though, and most of the time we mow in the hot sun, a cloud of dust and grass following us with the flies.

On this morning, the lakes are quiet, perfect sheets of glass. Careful not to get too close to the reedy edge, we circle the first lake. In the heat, I squirm in my seat, perched between his legs, watching where we are going, while he leans over the side and monitors the position of the wheels. Twice before, on different occasions, the tractor has been driven into the lake and as many times been towed out. The tall grasses and the uneven shoreline make it difficult to know where land ends and water begins. The possibility of slipping is great, even for the man who dug the sand with a backhoe and watched the water table rise and fill.

My grandpa says little as we ride. The engine noise and my place in front of him make conversation difficult though not impossible. When he wants to say something to me—ask me to shift my weight or hold on tight—he leans close and speaks directly into my ear. His words are moist and heavy, thick like the haze on the plains.

My place on the tractor, in between his thighs, pulled tight against his body, is a place of privilege. It brings with it the possibility of cash. My grandpa hands money to his grandchildren freely, even obscenely, pulling ten-dollar bills from his wallet like we pull fish from the lake, one after another, sometimes on a baitless hook, growing bored by the overabundance of crappie. Even as a child I recognize that he gives money in place of intimacy, or maybe, closer to the point, in exchange for intimacy. If I sit on his lap, let him hold me on his knees, tolerate the scratch of his day-old beard, I will be rewarded.

Within an hour, we finish the last loop around the lake and are riding the mower surveying our work. The grass is fresh and new, a slate of green. Still quiet, the house saddles the two lakes, the plate-glass window in the living room perpetually keeping an eye on things. A light in the kitchen suggests that coffee is made, but I cannot see heads moving around or life of any sort. The hum from the tractor remains steady, drowning out the cicadas and frogs, and we bump around the uneven ground, retracing the patterns in the lawn we cut just an hour before, returning to where we have already been.

He cuts the engine and we sit there, me between his legs, only the thick sound of tree frogs heard. My grandpa's hand moves under my shirt, rubs my flat chest, groping, stretching, circling around. Trapped between his legs, I don't move, even though I know what he does is wrong. He holds me and rubs me and then rubs some more.

I am still there, at the age of eight, on a tractor, in the middle of the lawn in a town that lies in the exact middle of the country, our household goods waiting for us in Washington, my books and toys wrapped in beige paper folded like origami, the Nebraska sun steady and hot, the back of my thighs slick with sweat and sliding along the vinyl seat, his purple-veined hand, wrinkled with age and worn from overuse, rubbing my chest, my shirt pulled up, leaving my belly exposed. He pulls me closer to his body, lingering on my nipples, never saying a word.

34

The Quarters

While Nebraska Plastics did run a factory there for years, Cozad was and is a farm town. In its heyday, neighboring townspeople would flock from miles around to Main Street on Saturday night for a movie and maybe a soda at the dime store. On those nights, the cars, parked in slanted rows down the middle of the street, occupied the length of the road. Everyone arrived brushed and scrubbed, necks burned from the sun, and decked in their finest, good overalls stiff against tired limbs. For a quarter you could buy a movie ticket, a bag of popcorn, and a licorice whip, a stunning array for a boy who was given one new pair of overalls a year.

Each week he earned the quarter not by an allowance but by shooting crows and taking them in lots of ten or more to town for a bounty. The blood-encrusted legs bumped against his thighs as he walked the Nebraska-straight roads, his mind on the movie he would see that weekend or the thunderheads in the distance. At home he collected the coins in a coffee can or a box or maybe even a sock that he kept under his bed, their heft a response to the poverty around him.

He and his brothers watched Westerns on those Saturdays— Red River, 3 Godfathers, Shane—movies where the good guys wore white, the bad guys, black, and the hero saved the day. Endings as tidy as the well-spent quarter. Sometimes it was a double feature, and they would beg their parents to wait just a little longer so they could see them both. Twenty-five cents seemed little to pay for the good guys to prevail.

35

The Drive

For decades my grandpa passed as a man with good business sense and a temper. He was a member of the Elks Club, played golf, could predict the weather based on the shape of the clouds gathered in the sky. When my Aunt Brenda finally spoke the truth, it broke the family, though I think no one could say we were surprised.

My grandpa died in 1984, when I was in high school and we were living once again in Virginia. Even before my grandpa's funeral, his body cold for a day—at the same time that we drove once again from Virginia to Nebraska without stopping, another thirty-six-hour trip, sleeping on the floor of the Dodge Caravan, my parents switching drivers without even pulling over on the interstate, my father scratching his arms until they bled, wearing a ring with a maroon stone I had never seen before, one that his father had given him, regretting the decision to put his father in a nursing home just weeks before, the guilt gathering in a puss-filled bump on the back of his head that my mother drained every two hundred miles while the car never slowed—possibly at that same time, my father's sister, Brenda, the chosen one, the girl with all the Barbies, described decades of sexual abuse she suffered, how the purple bedroom I had always coveted, the one specially designed for her, was a place of terror, how her own father, a man she should have trusted and loved, would force her to please him, would make her body move in a way no child's should ever know, how she had gone to her mother and been told to keep silent, been accused of lying, willed into further submission, how her older brother listened every night to the sounds coming from her bedroom and could not figure out a response, and how Brenda's allegations were followed by the stories of others in the family, my father's sister-in-law, someone he loved almost more than his own siblings, a young bride living with her in-laws, struggling to keep her husband's father from grabbing her in the kitchen, the shed, the long rows of corn, raping her, and then her daughters, the next generation, my cousins, with stories of their own, stories that were maybe told for the first time while we sped through Indiana and Iowa, my grandfather barely dead, the night concealing the fields of corn, my father buying McDonald's coffee by the Thermos-full, edging the speedometer ever higher.

36

The Horse

Seattle is never home. Even if rain hadn't fallen every day, turning yards into lakes, we only live there nine months, so roots are impossible. My father's graduate program starts the end of August, and my parents have little time to find a place to live. Our belongings need to be unloaded, my brothers and I registered for school. Maybe because we live in Seattle less than a year, just long enough for me to enter and complete third grade, or maybe because it rained so much I never got a good look at the landscape, it is the one place I lived as a child where I never learned the address. I can't even tell you the street our house was on, a year of my life lost somewhere in Bellevue.

I do make a friend in Seattle. She is a horse. Or at least she insists I treat her as a horse. Every day at recess, on the far side of the playground in a thicket of pine trees, Lori and I gallop atop a hill. We play far away from the other third graders, not eating lunch or snack in order to have more time.

"Your name is Fiery Chestnut," she says, "because your coat is red. You're reddish-brown with white around your hooves and forelock."

I nod, already preening the white cuffs on my coat, happy my mother has bought me a winter coat in a horse-possible shade rather than, say, a green one. I stand like a quarter horse, solid and lean.

"I'm Black Beauty because my coat is black. All black. You follow me because I'm the leader."

And with a toss of her equally dark hair, Lori heads for the next grove of trees on the other side of the playground.

"Neigh, neigh," I whinny in pursuit, my hands bent hoof-like in front of me, stamping the air. I don't know a thing about horses. Nebraska is full of cows and Virginia, trees. I haven't ever been close to a real horse, let alone ridden one. But I follow Lori, sweeping across the playground as rain clings to my chin and clumps in my hair.

We neigh around the trees, galloping between the wide-girthed pines that drop enough needles year-round to make cozy beds and piles of hay. Beneath the pine needles, beetles scurry, seeking shelter with our every sweep.

"A bad man is whipping us," she continues, now hiding behind a tree in our grove, far from the girls who never play pretend but spend recess cherry dropping from the high bar. "We have to run."

A bad man is always whipping us, always hurting us in some way, and our response is to run. We are horses after all. We don't talk. We neigh. And Lori narrates our every move.

"Here he comes," she cries. I gallop faster, still holding my hooves in front of me, my head bobbing up and down, snarling through my nose, my eyes gone white while I look from the side, waiting for Lori's next words.

Because I know so little about horses, don't own Lori's horse encyclopedia comparing the finer points on Arabians and Appaloosas, I simply copy Lori's movements. When she stamps, I do. I gallop, canter, and trot when she tells me.

"Get him!" she cries. "Get him!"

And I turn, with black-coated Lori at my side, to face our attacker. Together we trample the bad man, snorting, stomping our feet on his body, pine needles bouncing against the dirt, showing no mercy for every breaking bone.

And when she says he is dead, I shout out, forgetting for a minute that I am a horse. "We got him!"

In one recess, we can kill twenty bad men and still have time to brush our fur.

Lori's parents are divorced. I have seen her mother making out with her boyfriend on the couch. I can only guess what demons Lori grinds into the ground with her hooves. Under my own feet, I envision my grandpa with his wrinkled and veined hands, or the girls at school who put their lunch boxes on empty seats to prevent me from sitting with them, or the nurse at Fair Hill who wouldn't call my mother for me. I trample it all into the ground.

37

The Party

I should be at Lori's birthday party. Under my arm, I carry the plastic model of the black-coated horse I have picked for her, wrapped in bright birthday paper. My mother has even made a puffy bow for the top.

But we have gotten lost on the way to her new house. My mother drives in circles around the subdivision, passing the pool and the rec center again and again but failing to find the right house. We finally stop at the information building near the pool to ask for clarification. Before my mother can reach the desk, though, a woman my mother knows from my Brownie troop says she had just dropped her own daughter off at Lori's party. Relieved, my mother writes down the new directions and within minutes deposits me at the party.

Only it is a different Lori's house, a Lori I know from Brownies. Mean Lori. Not the Lori with strong hooves. Apparently two Loris are having birthday parties on the same day and in the same housing complex, and I know them both. I have been left at the wrong house.

What could Mean Lori's mother have thought when this uninvited eight-year-old shows up at her doorstep bearing a present? And why don't I say something to Mean Lori's mother or to my own mother or to Mean Lori herself? Why do I just walk in, hand over the gift, and make my way to

where the other kids are assembling in the living room?
Mean Lori, red-haired Lori, hates me. Yet, here I am at her
birthday party.

I cannot make a fuss.

While the rest of the children head to the backyard, I
remain indoors amid the dark, formal furniture, the thick
upholstery, and a couch with curved wooden feet that grab
the carpet. Near the cherry buffet, I note a dish that holds
candy. Outside, children take turns on the swings. When it
is time for cake and presents, I stand by as Mean Lori opens
the first Lori's present. As it turns out, she also likes horses,
so the gift is a hit. But I grow angry that my carefully chosen
present sits atop a pile of Mean Lori's cache.

Toward the end of the party, when everyone has gone
back outside, I am once again alone in the air-conditioned
living room. I slink over to the buffet, backing up against the
cold wood, and pretend to rest there. In the kitchen, Mean
Lori's mother runs water in the sink and moves dishes from
the counter to the cupboard. From outside, I can hear the
shrieks of the children, imagine their bodies swinging from
the monkey bars. I have no desire to be with them. Nor do I
want to be alone in the living room. The unwrapped horse
stands amid the other presents on a wide plain of crum-
pled wrapping paper. Sweat gathers in my armpits; my heart
beats fast.

When I hear Mean Lori's mother open the refrigerator, I
move my hand slowly behind my back. I feel for the edge of
the buffet, then the cool, shiny surface, then the glass bowl,
all cut angles and hard. It is difficult to reach behind my
back, my elbows pull at the joints, my shoulders ache, but
I can feel the tiny candies gathered in the bowl. The crinkle
of cellophane is the only sound in the room except for the

vented air pushed through the metal grates near the floor. At first, I take only one, but then, reconsidering, I grab as many as I can and quickly draw my hand back to my body. When I look down, I see six different candies in my hand, reds, oranges, yellows and browns, pinwheels of color. I close my hand around the candies just as Mean Lori's mother moves into the room.

"You will get some candy at the end of the party," she says, her voice stern and certain. She stands in the doorway, her hands red from the dishwater, her hair falling over her forehead. "Can you put them back?"

The candies slide easily from my sweaty hand back into the bowl. I look to the floor.

When the party ends, Mean Lori's mom hands me a goody sack filled with the same candies—all reds and yellows and blues. I can't meet her eyes.

"Did you have a good time?" my mother asks when I make it to the safety of the car.

I say nothing, only nod my head.

"Did you get a goody bag?"

I hand my mother the sack, and she takes a piece of candy out before pulling into the street.

"Black licorice," she says, "my favorite."

On the drive home, I am silent. When my mother prods, I say I don't feel well.

"Too much sugar," my mother says, nodding her head.

As the pines flash by outside the car window, I try to make sense of my actions. My cheeks burn with the memory of Mean Lori's mother standing over me. I know what I have done is wrong. But the thought of Mean Lori galloping her new black pony across the living room carpet makes me angry. A few stolen pieces of candy can hardly right the balance. Under the gray Seattle sky, gulls peeling from the clouds like falling stars, I fight to hold these competing feelings inside me. It is not unlike the moment I yelled at my father in the hospital, where pain and love and anger all collided together and left me hollowed out. I cannot sort them, cannot label them, cannot explain my actions. Instead, I say nothing during the drive home, count the light poles as we pass.

38

The Can

Moments exist, many moments—the majority, my father would say—where life unfolds happy and sweet. For me, such moments remain frozen like a thin sheet of ice, brittle, and not to be trusted. The ice could crack with my father's temper, my mother's call to clean our rooms, another fall, another burn, another move.

We are playing "Kick the Can" in the Seattle basement, the Coke can resting in front of the fireplace, my mother guarding it, as my brothers and father and I mount our attack.

Rain splatters the windows in the dark, winter evening, but our surges for the can keep us warm. We have eaten an early dinner, hamburger casserole with green peas and cheese-filled biscuits huddled like a family on the top. In the hour before bedtime, we often play Blind Man's Bluff or Hide and Go Seek, a time when my mother stops working, stops picking up the house or ironing or packing lunches for the next day. My father studies after we go to bed.

"Get the can," my father cries, hiding behind the rattan furniture with Bryan, drawing my mother to that side of the room.

Scott breaks for the can, but my mother grabs him and tickles him as his body drops to the floor in laughter.

"I'll get it," I yell, sure that I can sneak past her while she tackles Scott.

In these games it is often one against the rest—one person blindfolded and on their knees calling out "Marco" while the others stand on chairs or climb atop a closet shelf and whisper "Polo" through cupped hands, trying to deflect voices off the ceiling or walls.

When we play hide and seek, my father always chooses the same place to hide, a giant cubbyhole beneath Scott's lofted bed. We know he is there, every time, and every time when we open the door and he jumps out, we scream.

"You open it."

"No, you."

I MAKE MY lunge for the can, but my mother tags me before I can kick it.

"I got you!" she cries.

But then my father springs from his place behind the table and races for the can. Instead of the can, though, he scoops up my mother, light like petals, and sweeps her high in the air. Her feet kick and twist, and he spins with her in his arms.

"Morris," she laughs, "put me down, put me down!"

"Never!"

And then they are dancing, a waltz or a jitterbug or a lindy without music, some sweeping, twirling, secret dance. Down one side of the family room, toward the sliding doors that run wet with rain, and then up the other. Her feet never seem to touch the ground, and her head falls back against my father's arms, heavy from their dance.

"Me too, me too," I call, having forgotten the game and wanting what I see in front of me, the certainty, I know now, of their love. As a child, though, such a moment feels as slender as our time in Seattle. The exception, not the ordinary.

Scott knocks the can with one good kick into the fireplace where it rings like a bell.

39

The Needle

Just before we move back to Hawaii, the month my father graduates and the sun begins appearing during the day, my parents hire a babysitter for my brothers and take me out for dinner to the restaurant at the top of the Seattle Space Needle to celebrate my ninth birthday. I wear a long green dress with a sheer white pinafore of georgette and a velvet belt that is as deep a green as the cedars on Mount Rainier. My hair is cut to a shoulder-length bob, and I refuse to wear the glasses that allow me to see. It is the last year I will feel pretty.

That night we eat on a merry-go-round, the city spinning beneath us. Lights blink in yellows and whites, and my parents sit across from me, all mine.

"What do you want to eat?" my father asks. "Order anything."

"I don't know. What is there?"

My mother looks at the menu, her eyes made more blue by her blue eyeshadow, a small sapphire at her neck, dancing in the candlelight. "How about a hamburger?" she asks.

It doesn't matter what I eat. I am in a restaurant long after dark, wearing a belt made of velvet, across from both my parents who smile easily.

"A cherry coke," I say, "with no ice."

When it comes, I let the cherry soak in its lukewarm bath. Looking out the window, for once not streaked with rain, I imagine that we have broken free of the Space Needle and now wheel through the sky. Spinning through the night, no babies have been burned and no hands have raked my naked chest. My father wears a suit, his nails clean from months of not having to work on the house or car. His hands bear no scratches, his eyes no strain, and he never once mentions how expensive the menu is.

Instead, we talk about what activities the Brownie troop should undertake. Between bites of burger, I ponder sit-upons and lanyards, homemade soap, and no-bake cookies.

As we leave the restaurant, we pass an instant photo booth. My father suggests we have our picture taken. Perhaps the novelty appeals to him. We have never posed in a booth before. Maybe he feels the night should be marked, the night we threaded the needle, the eve of the nuclear race, months before he becomes a senior officer.

"You first," he says. And he sits me by myself in front of the empty white screen.

I wait smiling under a row of bangs curled tight for the evening, having just eaten a meal as I spun through the sky.

"Get in, Cynde," he calls to my mother, "quick before the next one." And then my mother slides beside me, the two of us laughing, caught only by the camera lens, there and gone, a glimmer, a glimpse, and then on to something else.

"Now, you," she laughs and pushes my father in, his newly grown mustache tickles against my face, and then he, too, is laughing, just as the camera snaps, no room left inside the booth, the two of us filling the frame.

The plan has been for the final picture to be the three of us. But the pictures come too quickly, the booth too small. My father tries to pull my mother back in, but she resists. "You go, you go," she laughs, "stay there," leaving my father and me together when the bright flash bursts for the fourth time.

In two minutes' time, a chain of tiny black and white photos issues from the side of the booth like so many pearls. The first shows me alone, front teeth uneven and in need of the braces that will come in a few years, smiling in the knowledge that I am not really alone. In the next, my mother is bending her head through the door of the booth, a smile to match. And then twice with my father, as if trying to emphasize the moment. Our heads in balance, our smiles wide, punctuating—in black and white—the night, an ending that is framed, happy, and right.

40

The Cave

We arrive in Hawaii in 1978—our second of what will ultimately be three tours of duty on the islands—not long before Ronald Reagan is elected. In very short time, Reagan will vow to "confront the Soviets everywhere," brand them the Evil Empire, and the Cold War will become a whole lot warmer. Jimmy Carter will prove an embarrassment to those in the military. The hostage crisis, my father will say, resulted from the president's unwillingness to allow the Marines to do their job. With Reagan, military spending will reach a level previously unimagined. My adolescence will span the height of the Cold War.

Having completed his master's in maritime law at the University of Washington, my father is now one of the navy's only international ocean law specialists. At a time when the Cold War is largely being waged underwater by nuclear-powered submarines, my father's knowledge about treaties and legal jurisdiction at sea is in high demand. That fall, I will help pin commander boards on his shoulders at a quiet ceremony on base, my mother smiling next to me, a ginger lei around her neck. My parents are thirty-eight.

WHEN WE DEPLANE the very first time back on the islands, having crossed the Pacific safely and clapping our thanks to the pilot, we are greeted by the soft, tropical air, so wet and thick our lungs require only half of it, leaving the rest for us to walk through.

We are greeted by the military community, just as we will, from then on, come to the airport to greet others. "Morris! "Cynde!" they cry. "Aloha!" "Welcome!" Then leis around our necks, a gentle kiss on the cheek, their skin smelling of PreSun and salt. We don't know any of them, but they carry our bags and ask about our flight as if picking up on a conversation we had been having.

Covered with flowers, we walk down the open-aired terminals of the Honolulu International Airport swimming in scent. We are surrounded by stone benches and the open sky as we pass gardens squeezed between boarding gates, Japanese lanterns and wooden bridges set among ferns.

"We're home," I hear my mother say to my father. They each wear so many leis—Vanda orchid, ginger and maile, pikake, lantern Ilima and tuberose, double plumeria—that I can't see their faces, just a mountain of flowers where their heads should be.

Home, I think, trying the word out, seeing if it fits. Breathing the scent of so many blossoms, candy leis filled with chocolate and li hing mui around my neck, welcomed by tanned and smiling people in Aloha prints, how can it be anything else?

I find out fairly quickly, though, that we don't actually have a home. People we have only just met drive us the fifteen minutes from the airport to Pearl Harbor and drop us off at Lockwood Hall, the hotel on base for officers. Because there are five of us, they give us the admiral's suite. We spend the next week in those two rooms, my mother terrified every time she turns her back that we will destroy the knickknacks—a tiny, silver F-16 balanced atop a metal post, a crystal dolphin, a set of woven coasters—gathered on every flat space.

Several houses are available and my parents arrange to tour them on the third day after our arrival. Even though I am nine, I am unable to watch my brothers for an entire afternoon, so my mother leaves us in a daycare just off base. What had felt familiar and welcoming with my parents close by becomes sinister in their absence. The mynahs no longer chat with me but screech my outsiderness from the nearby trees, and the palms rattle their fronds like a many-armed monster. The kids at the daycare are mostly locals, with darker skin and dark hair. They stare when we walk into the play yard. I look for anything I might recognize, but even the adults seem strange to me. The woman who leads us from our parents has thick, black hair she pulls back from her face and twists into a bun with a chopstick at the base of her neck. I can't imagine how a single stick can hold all that glossy hair in place.

The three of us spend the entire day sitting inside a concrete tube in the play yard, our backs against the curved wall, feet on the opposite side, a bomb shelter of our own. Bryan, only three, tries to leave several times, sees the sandbox, the swings, the other children, but I make him remain. In the coolness of the tube, I feel safe, and until our mother returns to get us, to take us to our new house and unpack our stuffed animals and toys, I am in charge. I gladly assume the role because its familiarity is a comfort amid all this confusion. Holding Bryan's pants so he can't escape, I pour bits of sand through his hands and roll a rock up and down the sides of the tube to make him laugh.

"We are pirates," I tell my brothers, "and this is our ship on the sea." It's a story my father often tells at night before bed. A magical tale of adventure and daring.

"I wanna swing," Scott says. Nearby, kids arc into the air, bare feet coated in sand.

"No, stay here. I'll tell a different story." I pull on his hand. "We are gypsies. We wander the world without a home."

Scott looks skeptical that I can rehearse the tale as well as my father, but he settles his body beside me.

"I have a sword," he says. And I arm us all.

In the darkness of the concrete tube we can be anywhere or nowhere. From the cool belly of cement, I can only see a slice of sky, blue with small puffy clouds. Sealed off from the outside world, safe, Scott listens to my story and Bryan buries his leg with sand, but their willingness to remain is temporary. Neither of my brothers understands that our family travels the world in a self-created capsule, constantly in motion, never to touch ground.

"We are three kids lost," I start a new story. "Our parents have left us alone. We live," I pause, conjuring my father's voice in my head, "on a houseboat and there is a whirlpool dead ahead."

At some point my mother's face appears at the end of the tunnel, the sun exploding behind her brown hair and creating a halo around her face.

"We have a home," she says, holding her hand out to my brothers who go to her eagerly, happy to be free.

"Yah!" Scott cries as he crawls out of the concrete tube on his hands and knees.

I want to go home, but realize I don't know what that means. In my father's stories, the orphaned kids survive because they stick together. They have no house, no yard, no mailbox. They do not need one. A part of me wants to remain in the cave, in the cubby under the bed, in the nurse's office, but another part wants to believe in the gypsy tale. I take my mother's hand.

41

The Skates

My parents choose a house in Maloelap, a military housing community for submariners. We are surrounded by captains of boats: The USS *Tunny*, the USS *Aspro*, and the USS *Indianapolis*. My father is the only man in the fifteen houses in Maloelap who doesn't command a boat of any kind, let alone a fast attack sub. While other fathers go to sea for weeks and months at a time to ping for Russians in the deep, my father heads for the office, telephone and pen his only weapons. I think both he and I suffer a kind of shame for not being real navy.

Looking at our house, no one would know my father doesn't captain a boat. All fifteen houses in Maloelap look exactly the same, single-floor square-shaped wooden houses, with a lanai at the center. They sit facing the street, at the end of long sidewalks, broad grassy lawns all around.

Like all military housing, the interior walls are military white, the floors, concrete with soft gray linoleum tiles, and the shrubs, low and close to the houses. Similar lawns, similar carports, the same blue signs in the yards identifying the name and rank of each sponsor. It is the military's effort to ease the stress of constant relocation. You could be anywhere. Virginia? Texas? Florida? The navy wants you to believe it doesn't really matter.

But military regulations can't keep a check on the natural world, and color returns with our arrival. White plumeria line one side of our house, dropping blossoms year-round. In the backyard, a blood-red plumeria and a trumpet tree. To reach our front door we walk under a canopy of bougainvillea, the purple blooms lit from inside. My mother grows tropical flowers in our lanai, birds of paradise, torch ginger, and heliconia; hibiscus hug the sides of the house, pink and red. The trees trade in multiple shades of green. Mango and banana, monkey pod and shower trees. Hawaii never dulls, not even in late November, when anthurium bloom just in time for Christmas.

AFTER THE FIRST few days in our new house, I am running around the neighborhood without shoes, my feet already toughening. Our yard has numerous trees to climb, a giant Hayden mango on one side and the trumpet tree in the back. Just one house down stands the Tennis Court Tree, an ancient shower tree with roots that push through the asphalt and a trunk thicker than my embrace. Much of my time is spent not just outside but up in the air, being tossed about in the branches, high above the houses.

Maloelap is also full of children. Within days, I meet Sandy. Both the oldest children in our families, Sandy and I move to Maloelap the same summer. Her house sits across from ours, back from the street in a hollow. The only girl my age on the street, our friendship is formed by proximity. We both wear eyeglasses with the round plastic frames sold at the Navy Exchange. We are the same height. The similarities end there, however. Sandy's face is dotted with freckles that become more prominent in the sun, while my skin browns easily, never burning. Her hair is red, matching her freckles.

The Hansen family has two more girls—Michelle and Ann—the same ages as Scott and Bryan. When my father finds out that Mr. Hansen was raised on a farm in Missouri the friendship between families is sealed. On weekends, we pile into our blue-and-white VW van and follow the Hansens' tan-and-white VW van to the beach. While Mrs. Hansen and my mother grow more golden in the sun, we head to the surf to play for hours, the sun tracking across the sky.

ONE AFTERNOON, SANDY and I are roller-skating in the thin hours after school and before dinner. My knees are already scraped from falls, when I follow Sandy into the cool of our carport, careful to avoid the oil spills.

"Pretend Han and I are making dinner," Sandy says, heading for the back of the carport and my father's work-bench. "Pretend you and Luke are coming over to see us and check on some droids."

I watch her red hair as she skates past me, feel just her fingertips brush my arm. Farther down the street, Scott and Bryan race on their Big Wheels. Every now and then, they spin out, scraping the asphalt, laughing. I still wear my uni-form top from school, a short-sleeved cotton blouse, the arm pits stained with sweat.

Sandy dictates our play, and Star Wars on roller skates is a favorite. Han and Luke don't exist except within our imagi-nations, two girls on Fireball skates talking to the air.

"All right," I call, shooting out from the carport, "Luke and I will go to Mos Isley and get some fuel," motioning toward the general area where I last stood with Luke.

We blast down the hill towards the stink pod tree, collecting enough long bean pods to keep a landcruiser running for a few days. My brothers wave to me as I shoot past. I chat with

Luke as I work my way back up the hill, calling him "Honey" and asking about his day. He is weary of fighting the Dark Side, whose powers seem to be growing stronger, and feels many disturbances in the Force. I make gentle understanding noises, suggest a bath and a good dinner. Then I consider wrapping my brown hair in ribbons that match my shorts, thinking I can sleep on the braids and have a "perm" the next day at school.

STAR WARS HAS only recently been released, with The Empire Strikes Back still about a year away. Sandy and I are obsessed. I have the movie memorized, collect the cards, and dream of days spent traveling the galaxy with Luke. The StarWars trilogy defines my teenage years as much as, and in accordance with, Reagan's own Star Wars, the Strategic Defense Initiative. In addition to its being another story of good triumphing over evil, I latch onto the movie for its predictability. While those around me see the movie again and again for the special effects or the cult following, I can sit in the movie theater and replicate my experience indefinitely. Nothing changes. If I look away for a minute, go to the bathroom, get more popcorn, I can re-enter the experience, pick it up like a dropped hat. No one dies who isn't supposed to. There are no wailing mothers with half-dead sons in their arms.

Plus, my father loves it, a modern-day western. And after he is promoted to commander, we see less of him at home again. At the movies, I can be with him for two hours and not have to worry that I might be doing something wrong. It's an approximation of intimacy that we both embrace.

Sandy is in love with Han Solo while I have my heart saved for Luke Skywalker. Sandy always chooses the bad boys—Ponch rather than Jon from *CHiPs* and Steven rather than Roy on *Emergency One!* I stay true to the good boys—they prove to me that if you do everything correctly you will win—but I wonder about those dark-haired ones, those that Sandy chooses, those who test the boundaries and still get the girl. Maybe because she attends public school while I am in a private one, or maybe because she has an older cousin named Kari who writes long letters from the mainland filled with adult details, or perhaps because her mother is a nurse and tells her things that I only read about in the magazines we steal from a bush near the tennis courts where sailors stash their porn, Sandy knows more about the world than I do. When we read in a *Playboy* about a meeting in a van on the side of the road that involves honey, it is Sandy who explains about tongues.

When Luke and I return from our mission, Sandy is lying on the ground rolling around. Her skates flop like dying fish on the grass, while she moans and holds her belly. It is immediately clear to me what has happened. While Luke and I were out, Sandy and Han have been "doing it" and now she is having a baby. She has at least one baby every time we play.

The neighborhood has grown quiet, as it always does in the afternoons. The mothers are inside, making dinner or cleaning up, the fathers not due home for another hour. Around six, a parade of cars will arrive, one khaki-uniformed man after another emerging from his parked car after he manages to avoid the bicycles and Big Wheels. Above, small white clouds trail across the sky, ending not far over the ocean.

"Ooooooh," Sandy groans, thrashing her skates around in the grass, "the pain, the pain."

"What can Luke and I do?" I ask, seeing that under her shirt she has stuffed the old cloth diapers my dad uses to check the oil in the car. She smells of gasoline and tires.

"Send Luke in the X-Wing to get Han. He went to the Vespera System to shoot Wamp Rats. I neeeeeed him."

With her last words, she begins to roll down the grassy slope in my front yard.

I give Luke a quick kiss and go to push Sandy back up the hill.

"Can I get you some water?" I ask. "A cool cloth?"

"No," she says. "Get some boiling water and rip some sheets!"

Sandy rolls back down the hill, and I return to the carport hoping to find some ratty diapers in the rag bin or maybe a bucket.

"It's coming!" I hear from the lawn only moments later.

Dropping the newly found bucket, I run over to her. She is breathing in short breaths and spitting everywhere.

"Whoosh whoosh, it's coming, whoosh whoosh, oh, the pain, whoosh whoosh, can you see the head, whoosh whoosh, oh Han, oh Han, where are you, whoosh whoosh."

I move to where I will be able to deliver the baby, and, with one final scream from her, I pull the rags out from under Sandy's shirt. She begins to weep.

"Boy or girl?" she cries, sobbing into the grass.

"It's a—"

"Boy! Han Junior," she says. "Oh quick, cut the cord."

I make a scissors motion in the air and hand her the rags. She holds them close, ignoring the fumes and the oil stains, muttering into the ball. When Luke comes home, he and I leave her and Han Jr. to go back out on patrol. But then my mother calls me for dinner.

I say goodbye to Sandy and skate up our sidewalk. I can hear the pans clanking in the kitchen, smell gasoline on my hands. Playing with Sandy is different from playing with Lori, the territory more treacherous. The physical act of trampling is something I can imagine, while "doing it" confuses and bewilders. But to be with Sandy, that bright flame of a girl, I am willing to pull rags from beneath her shirt.

42

The Record

One night, late into the summer, Sandy and I sit on the curb outside my house watching to see if a car will come by and squash the cockroach crossing the road. Scott and Michelle are building a tree fort on the side of the house, and the steady bang of their hammers punctuates the afternoon.

"What do you wanna do?" Sandy asks.

I look around. The neighborhood seems quiet except for the ring of the hammer. No one is even out mowing the lawn. Even though it has taken a solid ten minutes, the roach has reached the other side of the road safely.

"Want to spy on Scott and Michelle?"

"Nah."

"Play Barbies?"

"Nah."

I feel bored, as well, watching the roach. We both, I think, had hoped a car would squash it flat, white guts squirting from underneath its wings.

"Hey," says Sandy, all of a sudden excited. "Let's do the teeter-totter record."

She stands as she says this, the bits of twisted grass she had been twirling in her hands showering to the ground. I have to look up to respond. Several times in the past year we have tried to break *The Guinness Book of World Records* for longest teeter-totter ride, but have always failed. We don't even know if a teeter-totter record exists. The teeter-totter sits at the park not far from our house and near the Tennis Court Tree. We typically last an hour.

"We never stay out very long," I observe.

"This time we will," she says, brushing her hands of dirt.

Within fifteen minutes, I have collected my stickers and erasers and a bottle of water and am standing under a darkening sky at the park. Sandy meets me a few minutes later pulling a wagon. She has raided the pantry and has boxes of Triscuits and packets of sugared Kool-Aid stuffed in a pillowcase with a flashlight and some bendable straws. After we get settled, I check the official time, 8:10, and we assume our spots on either end of the metal teeter-totter, the sun only now sinking behind the horizon.

Up and down we ride for half an hour. Neighborhood kids stop by to see how we are doing, reminding us of the recent sighting of Bloody Mary as well as the tale of the bloody hook. I think I can see the hibiscus near the Thomases' house shaking, but I tell myself it is a cat and not a ghost. Every now and then, I take a hit from the Kool-Aid packet.

Soon the other kids are called in for baths or late dinners. One by one, the sounds of other children diminish and disappear. Even though Sandy and I have been alone in the park for some time, with each holler the space around me feels more lonely. At 8:45, I send Scott home with a message that I will be late for my nine p.m. curfew. I tell him to ask Mom or Dad to come to the park and renegotiate; so far neither has appeared.

Sandy and I teeter-totter in the now empty park while she talks about boys at her school. Each time I come back to the ground, I feel the earth beneath me for a second before pushing off. My rear end has grown sore from the metal seat, the insides of my thighs red and rubbed raw. I wrap my arms around my body and push off the ground without hands.

"Shit," Sandy says.

"What happened?"

"I dropped the damn Kool-Aid. It was strawberry. I was saving it."

I can no longer see her in the dark, but I imagine her high in the air, held aloft by my weight.

"What time is it?" she asks.

On my next meeting with the ground, I grab my watch, but I can no longer read it in the dark.

"I can't see it."

"Use your flashlight."

"I didn't bring one."

"You didn't bring a flashlight? How are we going to keep track of our record if we don't know what time it is?"

She has a point, but I had been so eager to make sure I had my entire eraser collection that I hadn't tended to the more practical.

"What about yours?"

"How can I give it to you? You're way down there."

"You could throw it," I offer.

The next thing I know the flashlight hits me in the head. I cry out, my forehead above my eye throbbing from the smack.

"Sorry," she says. "You told me to throw it."

We teeter-totter in silence for a while, my head gradually hurting less. I'm not mad at Sandy. I should have remembered a light.

A FEW STARS rest in the bowl of the sky, but the lights from Salt Lake Shopping Center wash out most of them. It has to be close to 9:30. I know I am going to be in trouble, but I don't say a word.

"I started shaving," Sandy says, after a long period of silence.

"What?"

"My legs. I shaved my legs. Last week."

In the darkness, I take in this new information, imagining Sandy's legs now longer and shinier, wondering how I could have missed such a thing while sitting on the curb.

"How'd you do it?" I ask.

"With a razor, dummy, how do you think?"

"No, I mean your mother."

Sandy's mother is known throughout the neighborhood as Mean Old Mrs. Hansen. As an adult, I realize she was just more willing to widen the boundaries of influence than the other mothers in the neighborhood. If you were within earshot of Mrs. Hansen then you were treated like one of her own: chastised and lectured.

Mrs. Hansen has told Sandy she couldn't shave her legs, but she has also forbidden make-up, a rule that Sandy circumvents by waiting until she arrives at school to apply purple eye shadow and frosted lipstick, Maybelline products she has stolen from the Long's Drugs at the nearby shopping center.

My mother has also said no make-up, and I obey. Cherry Lip Smackers lip gloss is all I am allowed. The one time I try to sneak to the Subase Movie Theater wearing blush, my mother catches me. I try to convince her that my cheeks are only sunburned and I have powdered them, but she makes me wash my face before we leave. How Mrs. Hansen doesn't see the rouge and mascara on Sandy's face when she walks home from school every day, I can't imagine. Maybe she is just too tired of raising three spirited girls while her husband is deployed on his submarine for months at a time. I know that when Mr. Hansen is at sea, they eat frozen dinners in front of the TV rather than sit-down meals in the dining room. Maybe the rule about make-up is equally affected by Mr. Hansen's presence or absence. Shaved legs, though, would be harder to hide.

"The first time I did it, I tore a huge gash in my shin," she says. My feet touch the ground and I push off, my body rising into the air.

"I didn't want my mom to find out, so I did it in my bedroom instead of the bathroom. I think it was because I didn't have any soap or water."

"What was?" I ask, confused.

"The bleeding. I think if I had used soap and water, it would have worked. Instead, I had this nasty scrape up my leg. It was bleeding everywhere."

In silence, I push off the ground again.

"The next time was just fine. I did it in the bathtub. No cuts."

I think of Sandy's slippery legs, how they must feel when she runs her hands against them. In the dark, I don't have to feel my own to know how hairy they are.

As if she can sense my thoughts, she offers, "You should try it. It's so much better than having hairy legs. Boys notice that kind of stuff."

I leave it to Sandy to tell me what boys notice and what they don't. In my world, boys notice nothing I do, ever, with or without shiny legs, but Sandy seems to suggest that with the right combination of actions, the right knowledge and understanding, this could change. At school the kids talk

about French kissing and giving head. They pass books like
Looking for Mr. Goodbar during history class. I ferry their notes
and pass their desires, but I don't participate.

"So will you do it?" Sandy asks.

I am not sure how much time has passed or if Sandy has
been talking the whole time. I notice that even the birds have
given up and gone to bed for the night.

"Do what?"

"Shave your legs," says Sandy, annoyed by my inattention.
She pushes off roughly from the ground, making me lose
my balance for a minute.

"I don't know. I think my mother would be mad."

"We can do it at my house," she suggests.

But I have been inside the Hansens' house, seen the inside
of their shower. "We can do it at mine," I say.

Scott comes to get me a few minutes later. "You're busted,"
he says, and I know I am.

"I gotta go," I say to Sandy. "My mom's gonna kill me."

To my surprise, she says she is bored anyway and wants
to get home to see Fantasy Island.

I pick up my erasers and stickers in the dark, then shake
Kool-Aid grit to the ground for the ants. Sandy loads her
wagon and starts to pull it down the path from the park. In
the light from the streetlights, I think I can see her legs shine.

43

The Shower

A week earlier, Sandy and I had sat with Mrs. Hansen in their living room, the walls around us covered with gold-filigreed drawings from Asia—a delicate white bird with a bushy pink tail, a pointed mountain lost in the clouds. Late in the afternoon, we were the only ones in the house, and, with the dark green drapes drawn, Sandy and her mother seemed to disappear into the equally dark couch. Sandy and I had spent the afternoon outside in the hot sun, roller-skating up and down the street, jumping a ramp made from a foraged piece of plywood. Sandy's knee bled. The air conditioner in the living room chilled the sweat on the back of my neck. Every now and then, the thick plastic covering the space between the air-conditioning unit and the window frame sucked and spat.

Mrs. Hansen was talking about "changes in your body," one of her favorite topics. I kept my eyes glued to my knees, scars and old scabs but no new blood. I hummed to myself in an effort to avoid listening. An ex-nurse, Mrs. Hansen felt herself an expert in all things body, and with three developing daughters at her disposal, she excelled in sexual maturation. Mrs. Hansen would be the one to convince my parents to buy me a copy of Dr. Charles Dobson's *Preparing for Adolescence*.

Mrs. Hansen would be the one to wrap a twelve-pack of Daisy disposable razors in Christmas paper and howl with delight when I unwrapped the pink razors at the neighborhood Christmas party.

Only a week ago, Mrs. Hansen had asked Sandy to take off her shirt so we could see her developing breasts. When Sandy refused, Mrs. Hansen turned to Michelle, her second daughter, who then clutched her romper top more closely. Mrs. Hansen didn't ask me; she knew nothing was there.

I hoped desperately that Mrs. Hansen wouldn't reveal her own ample chest to us, didn't want to know if the freckles that tracked the bridge of her nose were to be found elsewhere on her body. Instead, Mrs. Hansen reached for one of her nursing books and produced a drawing of a breast with the side cut away. Veins ran from nipple to the fleshy red meat of the breast. I turned away as heat surged to my cheeks.

"DID YOU HEAR me, Jennifer?"

I looked up from my knees at the red-haired woman sitting across from me on the sofa. Her legs were crossed, the flesh of her thighs dimpled and pocked.

Mrs. Hansen continued, not waiting for, or even apparently expecting, a response, "You have such pretty hair, but you never take care of it. It's all greasy and tangled." She sighed.

I tucked the failed feather partially behind my ears, the rest framing my face. It didn't feel greasy, and I liked how I could hide behind the curtain of bangs.

Sandy stood up and headed to the kitchen. "I'm hungry," she announced. "What can I eat?"

Mrs. Hansen ignored her daughter's question and unhinged her legs, moving forward on the couch. Her breasts swaggered beneath her t-shirt, two rumbling sailors under a tent. She glanced at me one last time, then stood up and offered her hand.

"Let's get this taken care of," she said.

I looked around the room, at the furniture and the framed prints, wondering what we were about to take care of. The tables stood polished and empty, the carpet recently vacuumed. I could see no mess, nothing that needed tending.

But the mess was me, and Mrs. Hansen took my hand from my lap, pulling me to stand. The plastic sheeting in the window thwacked in the afternoon breeze, and the condenser ignited into action.

She never asked me if I wanted a shower. I was never given the chance to say yes or no. As we walked down the dark hallway to the back bedroom, Mrs. Hansen still holding my hand, leading the way, I cast my eyes about for rescue. But the blinds were drawn against the sun and the doors to the rooms off the hallway, closed to keep the cool air in the living room. I might have fallen down a hole.

"Get your clothes off, while I warm the water," Mrs. Hansen said as soon as we reached the bathroom. Above me, the light shone hot and bright. Steam already tendrilled toward the ceiling.

I heard the button on my shorts ring as it hit the floor.

Mrs. Hansen didn't even glance at my body. She was too busy testing the water and folding and refolding a fresh towel she had taken from the linen closet. The casual talk of bodies, what the books said, what the pictures demonstrated, seemed to matter much less when there was an actual body to clean. I stood in the steaming bathroom with my arms wrapped around my nakedness, trying to cover everything, which was really nothing, at once. In the sink near the shower, I saw a glob of toothpaste and several dark hairs near the drain. Then Mrs. Hansen grabbed me by the hand and pushed me into the shower stall. The water ran fast and hot down my body, racing to the drain. Mrs. Hansen sighed, as if suddenly wearied by the job in front of her, and lathered a bar of soap. Steam billowed up from the floor of the shower. Then I felt Mrs. Hansen's hands as they scrubbed first my arms, then my shoulders, then my back, then moving down to my bottom and thighs.

In some small spot in my mind, a part that hadn't completely shut down when my clothes hit the floor, I wondered why Mrs. Hansen was so concerned with my arms and back instead of my hair. But that thought went the way of the soapy water, leaving me naked and alone while Mrs. Hansen drew a bar of Ivory down my thighs. With each vigorous scrub, each lathered handful of suds, I shrunk deeper into the steam. I imagined myself clothed in its warmth, hidden behind its white curtains. Tears mixed with water and shampoo and shuttled down my face. I stopped tracking the route of Mrs. Hansen's hands.

"See," said Mrs. Hansen, as she drew her fingers across my scalp, "hair so clean it squeaks."

When she finally offered me the towel, I clutched it to my body. She left me in the bathroom where my skin beaded with water and then hummed her way down the hall. I put my dirty clothes back on. They were warm and soft. Within seconds, my t-shirt grew damp along the shoulders as water dripped from my hair. The moisture soaked further into the fabric, widening the ring of wet.

44

The Dog

I wake in what seems to be the middle of the night, the plumeria outside my window just a shadow. The neighborhood kids have left the curb for bed, leaving the night quiet but for the crickets and the sough of the trade winds. Perhaps a noise wakes me, or a bad dream. Perhaps I want a drink of water from the bathroom tap. Or perhaps I know on some deep level that I am alone. I get up. The lights are on. The furniture, the random shoes, the newspaper folded by my mother's chair appear as they did when I went to bed. Even the TV remains on, as if someone has gone for a snack during a break in the evening news. I call and call for my parents. No one is there.

From the kitchen to the family room and back into their bedroom, I run from room to room searching for them. In the showers, under the beds, behind the closet doors, I look for them as I have been taught by my mother to look for lost shoes or a necklace—thoroughly, by retracing your steps, and by picking things up. After a few minutes, I return to the murmuring television. Maybe, I tell myself, my mind casting for possibilities and panic metastasizing, they are running an errand. Milk, I reason, or breakfast cereal. Even as I rationalize their absence, though, I know they are dead. I know with the same certainty that I knew upon awaking that I was alone. Within minutes, I am already testing the shores of orphanhood.

I go outside.

Stars are what I remember. So many stars scattered above me. I am seldom awake to see the night sky. Even in my panic, it is the beauty of the night that I first notice. Standing on the sidewalk, the trade winds worrying my nightgown like water about my knees, I look up and down the road for my parents but am met by emptiness. I think of going across the street to the Hansens' house to see if my parents are there. Maybe they are playing games, or talking, or planning our next camping trip. Maybe my parents are but footsteps away. As if by magic, at the very moment I turn my gaze across the street, the last light in the Hansens' house, the bedroom lamp, I suppose, goes dark. I could be the only person alive in the world.

Turning back towards my house, I think to call the Hansens in hopes they can reassure me that all is well. An adult will know what to do. When I reach the door, however, I realize that I have locked myself out. Cold and scared, palm leaves rattling like skeletons, I do what I can. I break a window and unlock the door. That I still believe my parents might return is evidenced by the fact that I leave a note saying I can explain about the window. Unable to remain in the living room where the lights reflect their absence, I return to the darkness of my bedroom and sheets still warm from my body. My brothers remain asleep in their beds. By the time my parents come back from their walk, I have wound the sheets around me like a bandage and lie sobbing in my bed.

For the next several years, whenever my parents try to leave me alone, I beg them not to go, throw myself on the floor, grab their legs. When they insist on seeing their friends, I call over to the Hansens several times a night asking to speak to my mom or dad. Hearing my mom on the phone—the metallic click of her earring against the ear piece, laughter in the background mingling with the shuffle of cards—is almost enough to calm me. And these calls are tolerated for a while. Soon, though, Mrs. Hansen begins refusing to bring my parents to the phone, tells me they aren't there, that they have gone to Waikiki, that I need to go back to bed. On these nights I sit in my bed and look out my window into the backyard, the plumeria a monster, the lights from across the valley very far away, and will them to return.

45

The Salt

Maybe your mother doesn't whisper "Home" to your father as you walk down the terminal of the Honolulu International Airport when you return to the islands for the second time. Maybe she is simply trying to remember the names of the people around you. Maybe she is telling him that she needs to stop at the restroom. Maybe you tell yourself that you have come home because you have grown tired of telling yourself you are only passing through.

A few years ago, you came across one of the diaries you kept on and off between the ages of eight and fourteen. On the last page, the names of the friends you played with during that particular tour of duty came together to form a list with addresses. It was your attempt to keep track of those the military asked you to leave behind. Two names appeared without addresses: Suzette and Kate. It is not that you did not know where they lived. Rather, it was that at the time of this diary you had not left them yet. In recording their names, you prepared for the fact that in a year or so they, too, would be left behind. They entered both your diary and your life as an absence.

Cut your losses, shed names like furniture and other heavy items to make weight, host a yard sale, get rid of your dry goods, remain light and mobile because you never know when you will have to leave again. Moving, moving, nothing remaining, the possibility of misplacing a box, your friend, a daughter seemed so great. Every summer the moving trucks would bring new families into the neighborhood and take others away, men walking up and down silver ramps carrying arm chairs as if they were baskets of fruit. You sit on the curb half-expecting the parents and children to spill from the truck along with their household goods. For the longest time you think the military function called the "Hail and Farewell" is one word (Halenfarel), a useful word that means both coming and going, a way to abbreviate what happens so regularly. Some days you spend the entire afternoon at the airport, seeing one family off and another in, carrying plastic bags filled with plumeria leis you strung hours before, coaxing the petals with droplets of water to remain fresh a little longer.

Being in the military means that the cupboards in your kitchen are always full of other people's dry goods. Things your mother never would have bought at the commissary: raspberry Jell-O, dried manicotti shells, unfamiliar brands of baking powder. Refugees from the shelves of neighbors who had recently relocated to military bases in other parts of the country. They have the feel of the exotic. You marvel at how your mother would transform the tubes of pasta into something more familiar, slip the Jell-O into a cake mix without your ever knowing it was there. Slowly the supply would dwindle and with it the memory of the family that had left the goods behind.

In turn, you, too, gather the staples that you could not finish before moving and load them into the red wagon to carry across the street to neighbors. Sometimes you wonder if you aren't all just circulating the same items, a box of

Carnation dried milk and a half-used bag of cornmeal uniting military families more strongly than any shared sense of duty.

When you have given away your dry goods, you know that the end is near. Clean the house for final inspection, a few days in a hotel and then off to a new state, a new house, a new school. Maybe for this reason you always feel protective of the things your neighbors give you. Though the items are often unfamiliar, you know what they mean for those who have just given them up. Continually asked to leave things behind, you become attached to salt.

46

The Wave

"The ocean," my father says the same spring I wake to find my parents gone, "has an order of its own." We are standing in the surf on the North Shore of Oahu, at Waimea Bay, brown-skinned boys with Boogie boards running past us to meet the waves. To be safe, he intones, you need to understand how it works.

On our first tour of duty in Hawaii, those years in Hospital Point when I was three, four, and five, I was fearless in the water, riding surf that kept adults on the shore. Topless, skin tanned from weekend after weekend at the beach, I would run into water well over my head and ride the backs of waves like ponies into the sand. I look at pictures of me at five, eyes squinting tight against the Hawaiian sun, standing at the edge of the surf, holding my pail and shovel like a sword and shield.

The girl in the picture looks as if she belongs to the water, bare skin covered in white sand, hair flying in the offshore breeze. Her parents could not pull her from the sea. Late in the day, the sun already setting, she would still be lying in the surf, rooting her hands deep into the wet sand to keep the waves from carrying her ashore. Water and sand moved around her and through her, in her hair and ears, sloshed in her belly, gathered between her toes and the creases in her thighs. She remained in the cooling surf as long as she could.

But that was before she understood that water could also take you down, bloat your body, transfigure you into an angel. That it could scar your skin. That was before she learned how easily one could fall, be split in half, the world never fully unified again. When that girl returns to Hawaii, she is full of fear. The waves that crash on the shore and swirl around her ankles seem to embody the very chaos she feels inside.

"It's only water," her father says.

But she knows all that water can take.

STANDING IN THE shallow surf of Waimea Bay that morning early in the spring, my father teaches me the first and most important rule of the sea. "Never turn your back on the water," he says. And he shows me by standing sideways in the knee-deep ocean, just at the point where the bottom makes its first drop and the waves tumble over one another before scrambling up the shore. His white undershirt, the same one he wears every day under his uniforms and now uses to protect his skin from the sun, is flecked with sand and clings to his chest. I stand beside him, fighting to hold firm against the surf, as my feet sink deeper into the sand with each wave.

"The ocean can change dramatically," he goes on to say, "and without warning. See that wave, that one not more than a bump on the horizon? It could become ten feet tall in seconds." I have no idea which of the waves he is pointing at, try to imagine the entire ocean exploding into a wall of water, thinking it would matter very little if I have my back to such a wall or not. Nevertheless, I remain sideways in the surf, trusting my father, hoping he will make it all okay.

"Never show it your back," he says.

When I look up at him, he says, "Like this." Then he clamps my chin between his fingers and turns my head back to the sea.

The waves are fairly low that afternoon, the pounding surf of winter months behind us. A broad bay on the North Shore of the island, Waimea is a good place to learn about the water. In the summer, the surf is easy and gentle, gradually building in the fall. Winter brings monstrous waves, as well as the big-wave surfers.

Scott sits on the shore near us playing "rock" in the foamy leavings, and I wish I could be with him. I love playing "rock," a game we think we have invented but that I realize much later in life is the natural inclination for every child at the shore. "Rock" requires no rules, holds no danger. All you have to do is sit in the surf and allow the wave-ends to push you the length of the beach or toss you along with the bits of shell and other sea debris. It is like being in the ocean without having to be in the ocean. Stranded high along the surf line after a particularly big wave, salty skin drying fast and taut in the sun and surrounded by dried kelp and scalloped shell halves, I always felt joined to the ocean even as it retreated. By the end of the afternoon, my bathing suit would hang heavy, the crotch filled like a marble pouch with sand that I would take home only to dump on the bedroom floor when I changed. Part of the sea slept beside me those nights and could be felt underneath my feet in the morning.

But you can't snorkel on the shore. You can't body surf or Boogie board or do any number of things we do one weekend after the next. "Rock" is okay for five-year-olds, but not for eleven.

"You have to get in the water," my father said at dinner the night before he took me to Waimea Bay.

"But I'm scared," I said.

"That's why I'm going to teach you the rules."

What happened when individuals failed to respect the water was evident every weekend at the beach. I would sit with my father on the sand and watch as the inexperienced tourists with impossibly pale skin, tried to hop waves like they might puddles, turning to friends on the beach to wave, leaving their backs so vulnerable my toes would curl toward my stomach. "Look there," he would say, "trouble."

Within minutes the tourist would find himself tumbling madly up the shore, arms and legs flailing, bathing suits drawn to his ankles like a flag of surrender. Sometimes lifeguards would have to rescue these people, often because they had ignored the signs signaling dangerous surf or rip currents and found themselves literally and figuratively over their heads. Sometimes my father went in after them.

47

The Wave

After standing sideways to the surf for a few minutes, my eyes never leaving the horizon, tiny waves pulling at my knees, my father holds me by the arm and takes me deeper. The water is cold, but that isn't what makes me catch my breath. As we move down the slope of shore we have been standing on, we enter the space where waves are breaking. They are still small, but if one were big enough it could put me into the "washing machine."

I stand on my tiptoes, hold my hands above the water.

"Dad," I say, worried, tears in my voice.

"Count," he says.

Waves arrive in sets of seven, he explains, and within each set of seven the waves increase in size, the next always bigger than the last. In addition, each set of waves also increases through seven sets of seven, the forty-ninth wave, then, being the largest of the series. "Always know where you are in the count," he tells me. Together we chant with the surf, "One, two, three."

The rules of the sea.

At the end of the seventh wave, like magic, the waves subside, a tiny ripple wandering up the sand.

We dive into the water. I can feel the salt stinging at the corners of my eyes. My father's warm body is close by; his leg brushes mine as he kicks himself forward. We pop up past the breaking point, treading water. Above us the sun burns hot, already turning the salt on our cheeks white.

IT IS ONLY later, maybe that night at dinner, or another day altogether that he tells me about the rogue wave, the *kahuna*, the one that will take you down, pull you out, roll you over, like the spotted body of an eel bursting from its hole.

"The *kahuna*?" I ask.

"It's Hawaiian for chief. The big one. You always have to watch for the *kahuna*."

TO KEEP A casual eye out for the *kahuna* is easy advice for my father to dispense. Even though he is a tall man, my father's body is like a raft in the ocean: it simply will not sink. When he scuba dives, he carries the weight two people would normally share, and even then he has to expel the air in his lungs in order to sink to the bottom. As a child, when I was first learning to snorkel, I would hold onto his arm as we skimmed the surface of the sea, his giant black flippers propelling the two of us with one small kick. Typically, one or both of my brothers would be on his other arm, and I imagine now this man, stretched like a cross, trailing children like kite tails.

We could stay for hours in the water, watching schools of fish duck and turn, their bodies flashing like so many mirrors, the plankton gathering in drifts, sunshine filtering through the water in forests of light. Sometimes my dad would leave us bobbing on the surface as he dove down to the reef or the sandy bottom. He could remain underwater forever, moving in and out of the coral, turning up rocks, threading his body through holes in the reef that seemed much too small for his large frame. As an adult, I would learn that such conservation of air was the mark of an experienced diver, one who felt as comfortable under the water as on land, but as a child it seemed a miracle that he could stay below so long. I would float over the bubbles made by his descent, letting them collect and break against my bare stomach, waiting to see what treasure he would pull to the surface—a spiny urchin, a sea cucumber, or an octopus rustled from his cave in the reef.

When he tells me that the ocean follows an order, that it abides by certain sets of rules, I believe him. This is a man who places starfish in my hands.

48

The Wave

Almost a year later, we are at Waimea again, on a day when the waves have turned wild from a storm in the Aleutians. One look at the surf, and I decide to remain on shore. The brew is fraught; I don't see a way to count the sets. One wave pounds in on the back of another, never giving pause. The foam mixes with sand, evidence of the ferocity with which the water is hitting the bottom.

"Come on," my father says, already headed for the water, sunblock still white on his face and shoulders. "It looks great!"

I am aware of the excitement in his voice, the childlike glee at being at the beach with the waves breaking just so.

"It's perfect for body surfing."

I remain unconvinced, even as he sweeps his arm toward the water, taking it all in.

"Just come on. I'll show you." An edge appears in his voice, replacing the glee, a change in tone barely perceptible, I imagine, to outsiders, but one that registers in my stomach.

I remember one night earlier that year when my parents had taken us snorkeling. We were staying in a beach cabin at the Barber's Point Naval Air Station and only had to walk a few yards from our door to the sea. The water was as black as the sky only without the encouraging pricks of starlight.

Standing on the shore, holding my mask and snorkel, I could not recognize the body of water that only a few hours before had nursed me along its shore. Flashlights only made things worse. The weak beams illuminated the salt and plankton, turning the blackness into a murky chaos. We had swum just a few yards before my brothers and I insisted that we return to the shore.

"Don't be silly," my father said, treading water, "it's the same water as it is in the day."

"I can't see," I said. "Something might get me."

"Don't be ridiculous. You know what's here."

Scott began to whimper with me.

"I want to go back," I cried, lifting my mask from my face and breaking another rule of the sea.

"Keep your mask on and stop being emotional. Use your head, Jennifer. It's fine."

But I was crying too hard by then.

We returned to the shore, and he roughly gathered the gear together. In the dark it was hard to see the black fins and booties. We would rinse them with fresh water when we got back to the cabin. My father's silence was almost enough to make me try again. I looked out at the liquid black water and imagined the kinds of creatures that might roam the sea at night. "All the animals come out at night," my mother had first said as we wiped saliva in our masks and prepared to enter the water. "Just wait."

But the inky ocean was too dark, the task too difficult, even if it meant resecuring my father's good humor.

NOW MY FATHER waits, squinting his eyes against the sun. Bryan sifts sand off to the side, a fine white curtain falling to a pile between his knees.

Reluctantly, I take off my shorts and follow my father down the beach.

"Don't forget sunscreen," my mom says, but my father is already leading me by the hand.

"THERE'S A POCKET," he says once we reach the shore, people walking past us, a boy chasing after his skim board and catching a ride on only inches of water. "You have to dive for it, but it's always there."

I look at the bay, a thumb-shaped outcrop of rock on one side that people scale to jump the twenty feet into the water, and imagine hundreds of Levi pockets resting on the sandy bottom alongside the shells and fluttering kelp, fish darting in and out, a snap for easy closure. But he is talking about something different, I soon realize, a pocket of safety, a pocket of calm. He shows me by running into the surf, into the face of a wave that threatens to crush him, and dives, plunging into its heart. Seconds later, the wave now spent at my feet, he pops up in the calm water, waving as he makes his way back to me.

Back on the shore, his smile broad and confident as if he has just made a rabbit appear from a hat, he says, "You dive."

"Die?"

"Dive. When the wave is too big," he says, holding his hand at shoulder-level, salt water dripping from his nose, his ears, the hair at his neck, "just dive for the pocket, let the wave roll over you."

"But how can I find it?"

"You just have to trust that it's there."

At that, he turns and runs straight into the five-foot waves. It looks like the wave will break right on top of him, crash down around his ears, but at the last minute he dives down. The wave consumes his body.

My father appears again at my side. "Did you see me?"

I nod.

"See how you just dive like an arrow under the wave?"

I nod again.

"Okay, now you try it."

Another skim boarder slides past us, the board slipping out from under his feet and flying into the air. I assume my mother sits with Scott and Bryan far up on the beach, filling plastic buckets full of sand.

"You have to go deep, though," my father says. "In the biggest surf, to the bottom is best. Try it."

Standing in the shorebreak of Waimea beach, I take a few steps toward the churning brew. All around me, people are catching waves and riding them into the shore, as well as tumbling like rag dolls in the washing machine of surf. I see arms and legs roll past me, a black-haired boy shoot through a tube.

The water is up to my thighs and I feel the shore slope away as I make my way into the frenzy. Things begin to happen quickly, giving me no time to count or to recon-sider or to even hold my balance. First the pull against my body into shore, then the pull back out, me in the trough in the middle, trying hard not to cry. One current grabbing my feet, the other pulling my torso.

All goes silent when the first real wave rises before us, assuming its proper size and form, the one it has been nursing for hundreds of miles as it rode across the open sea. Rising from the chaos of the shore, it sucks the water away from my body. I can no longer touch the bottom, somehow having been pulled deeper into the sea. The wave draws me close, pulls me under its lip.

"Dive, dive," I hear my father yell.

I feel the pressure around me, the force of the water. Others are shrieking in joy. It is a great wave. They jostle their bodies to position themselves for the ride, while all I can think about is the shore. My heart races and the tears come steadily now. I want to look back at my father, have him help me, but I keep my eyes on the ocean, knowing he will be angry if I turn my back on the sea.

Just as I feel the lip thunder above my head, I dive, down into its heart, into the blackness. I don't think about rabbits or Levis or whether my feet will get caught by the lip of the wave and whip me back out. I just dive. Down, down, down. And then I find calm, smack in the middle of chaos. The change registers in the quiet more than the forces pulling at me. I can almost make out the tiny pops and clicks of sea animals and bits of shell shushing in the surf.

It isn't an easy calm, though. I have to work for it, have to lobby against the physical properties of salt water. Above me the wave charges and boils. The pressure pushes down, though the threat feels distant. Every now and then water-wave tendrils grab at my ankles and hands, trying to draw me into the ocean's mighty works. But the wave eventually passes, and I pop up to see my father clapping his hands on the shore, shouting, "Hooray! You did it!"

When I come out of the water, my father gives me a hug. His wet t-shirt feels cold against my skin, but his body is warm. "See," he says. "I told you."

49

The Wave

Soon I become the girl in the pictures, the fearless one riding waves like horses into the shore. Maybe not as intrepid as when I was four and five, but brave nonetheless. I can spend an entire afternoon snorkeling with my family, hours swimming under my own power in water forty or fifty feet deep. I ride a Boogie board in rambunctious surf, race my father to the shore. I might even be able to snorkel at night, though my father never offers to take me again.

The fall I am twelve, we go with the Hansens to Waimea one Saturday afternoon. Our mothers set up beach chairs that they will rotate with the sun, and the six kids have free range on the shore. By then, all of us can swim well, and even Bryan can ride a Boogie board like a pro.

That day the waves are already anticipating the winter season. They form perfectly just after they enter the bay, and then rise to four or five feet before crashing into the shore. Sandy and I are out playing in them, or really beyond them, in the deep but quiet space past the breaking surf, where you can bob up and down on the swells just before they drag the ocean floor and crest. But being out that deep means treading water constantly. At the end of the last set, Sandy decides to go in. I can see her orange bathing suit as she makes her way up the beach.

I am tired from diving under the waves, but for whatever reason I am not ready to leave the ocean. The water feels cool on my body, in opposition to the sun that beats a steady rhythm on my scalp. The waves are getting larger, cresting sooner, and I am having to dive more often. Sometimes, the waves come in so quickly, I have to stay in the pocket for the length of two waves.

On the shore, I can see my parents and the Hansens sitting on their orange beach chairs watching the surf. I think about trying to get in, but the waves are already too big and I make the decision to wait the set out. Because waves can be so deceiving in the way they rise from nothing, the horizon gives no hint as to where we, the ocean and me, are in the series. Somewhere in the midst of having lost count, the treading and diving, the wish to be on the shore, the kahuna rises. A moving wall of water, when before there was nothing. All around me, I watch as people get sucked toward the monstrous wave, and I feel my own body pulled. I wonder if, when I look down, I will only see the ocean floor because all the water will have been taken to make this wave.

Waiting until the very last minute, until the kahuna has consumed most of the water around me to feed its growing body, until its lip has thrown a shadow over my head, I plunge beneath it and head for the pocket. I know I need to swim extra deep to be safely out of this wave's grasp, so I go as deep as I can, my ears aching with the pressure. I search for a coral head or a bit of reef, something to hang onto, but I can't make it to the bottom. When I find the pocket, the place where the roar of the wave diminishes, I no longer feel like I am being consumed. There I wait, the body of the monster moving over me like a powerful spell of nausea. Inside the

wave, I count out of habit, not sets but seconds. And I wait
and wait for the pummeling and pressure to pass.

But it doesn't. The wave remains, or the remnants of the
wave, or a second wave, or a third. Try as I might, I cannot
get back to the surface. Each new attempt is met by frothing
swirling bubbling water pushing me back to the bottom.
Panicking, I open my eyes in the salt water. Through the sting
and blur, I see only what my body has already told me, the
turning storm of white water. I rack my brain for something
my father has told me, a way to get a breath when unable to
reach the surface, a route out of the wave when every exit is
blocked. But I have nothing.

Finally, after what seems like a lifetime in darkness and
frenzy and a last struggle toward the sunlit surface, I break
through the remains of the wave and find air. My lungs burn
as I take a breath. The beach is cleared of people like the
streets after a summer rain, everyone, including my family
and the Hansens, have run for higher ground. They stand, refugees, clutching half-soaked beach chairs and open coolers.
The water's surface still fizzles with bubbles. Not a wave in
sight, the ocean spent, I swim for the shore.

MY FATHER DREW lines on water and regulated travel for the
naval fleet guarding the Pacific. He determined the limits of a
country's legal jurisdiction, the rules of engagement between
ships at sea, the procedures necessary to keep straits and
gulfs violence-free. As an adult I have often wondered how
my father felt to be the one charged with legislating a body
that covers two-thirds of our planet, a body that never ceases,
never stills, but rather roams the earth's surface in search of
another shore upon which to hurl its feathery edges. Would
he lie awake at night, briefs and opinions coursing through

his mind, and shake at the futility of his task? Or did the rules never fail him? Though I also realize this can't be true. He looked for syringes that he knew were broken, brought a hammer down on his pet pig's skull, drew his knife against another boy. The rules have failed us both.

50

The Cowgirl

My body's first betrayal arrived with the rain, when I was ten.
That October the skies flooded Oahu, threatening the post-
ponement of Halloween. Gutters rushed with water, carrying
cigarette butts, plumeria, and plastic spoons. Water seeped
under the floorboards of cars and swelled the surf. In spite
of it, my parents let me attend the Subase Chapel Halloween
party with Sandy and her younger sister, Michelle. We were
left, a cowgirl, a ghost, and a tube of Crest toothpaste, at the
Quonset hut that doubled as Sunday school, the car lights
blinking in the rain as my parents drove away.

For an hour we played games—bobbing for apples, pin the
broom on the witch. Because her Crest costume came down
to her ankles, Michelle stumbled through musical chairs.
Between events, I carefully ate an orange-frosted brownie,
not wanting to spill anything on my cowgirl outfit before
the costume contest started. The tin Quonset hut was warm
and wet with our bodies by the time the adults called for the
contestants. Soon my parents would be returning.

When it was time for the contest, in groups of five, we
were taken into the judging room—a room that served on
Sundays as the classroom for the preschool-aged children
where they colored pictures of Jesus walking on water or

feeding the five thousand. The small plastic chairs had been moved to one side of the room creating a large empty space where each contestant had to stand before the judges.

I didn't know the other kids in my group but felt proud in my costume. My mother had made it for my birthday a year ago. Even though I had only lived in Texas six weeks, I felt that a cowgirl was something I was—or could be—that one should be a cowgirl if she were from Texas. So I had asked my parents for the outfit along with Shaun Cassidy's *Born Late* album. I received both. The costume consisted of a fringed vest and matching fringed skirt made from blue denim, guns and a holster borrowed from my brothers, and a red hat with white loops running along the band. The only problem was that I had to pee.

If I had thought about it, I would have remembered that there were bathrooms in the building, but, for some reason, on this night, I had forgotten where they were and was too afraid to ask one of the adults for directions, too embarrassed.

The line was moving slowly, and nervously I twined my legs and gently bounced whenever we would stop. Finally, it was my turn. I entered the judges' room. Immediately the need to pee left me as I saw that one of the judges was none other than Blair Basset, the dreamy son of our choir teacher and the one who played piano for our performances. I had been in love with Blair Basset since forever by this point. While he had no idea who I was, he had and would continue to inhabit my world for the next few years. Long after I stopped going to Subase Chapel, long after Blair would leave for college, I would give his name as a possible future husband along with Luke Skywalker, the gentle Roy DeSoto from *Emergency*, and Captain Apollo from *Battlestar Galactica*.

As I stood in the middle of the room, before the judges and audience, it was Blair who spoke to me, a brown-haired girl in her cowgirl costume.

"Tell us what cowgirls do," he said.

The judges waited.

I peed on the floor.

Leaving a puddle where my boots had been and looks of surprise on the faces of the judges, I ran to the bathroom. Suddenly I knew right where it was. No one came to help me, or maybe I insisted I was okay. I have no idea who mopped up the puddle. Alone, in the bathroom stall, I stuffed a wad of toilet paper into my stained and wet underwear, trying to keep everything okay. My thighs itched and the toilet paper grated against my skin, but I was able to make it outside without being seen, where I sat down on the curb, the rain having stopped, and waited for my parents. At home I buried my wet underwear in the laundry basket and pretended it never happened.

51

The Boxes

"Boxes," my father said to me, when I was sixteen, in the days immediately after we had moved from Virginia back to Hawaii again and with only two weeks' notice. I had just started my junior year of high school in Virginia when Admiral Lyons ordered my father back to the Pacific. I cried for days, in big dramatic outbursts meant to hold my father accountable for my suffering. It was 1985, and we were living in the Hilton Hotel because no housing was available on such short notice. That afternoon, I stood on the balcony outside our rooms and passively threatened suicide by questioning the rate my body would fall if I hurled it from that distance.

Tired of standing, I took a seat in a plastic webbed chair across from my father, my legs folded against me. Salt-softened air from Waikiki brushed against us both, the wind in my hair. I was tired of trying to make friends.

"When something bad happens to you, Jennifer," my father said from his chair, a can of Coors sweating in his hand, "something that wants to hurt you, that makes you sad, you simply think of your mind like a dresser." He pointed to his head, his fingers bent not unlike a gun. "A dresser full of drawers. And you take the bad thing, the memory, the loss, whatever it is, and you put it in the drawer of the dresser. Envision yourself doing this, like you were packing clothes in there. Then you shut the drawer and lock it. You lock it. Do you hear me?"

I nodded my head, though I wasn't really listening. I had heard his theory of locked boxes my entire life. Any time I didn't "act rational," any time I "let my emotions get in the way," he brought out the dresser, told me to imagine just throwing the key away.

Briefly, I considered what must pain my father, what must be locked inside his own chest of drawers, or if he even had one. He seemed too tall, too strong, too confident for me to imagine how his own life might come undone.

"Don't look in the boxes," he continued. "Ever. Or maybe not ever, maybe later you can, but then only peek, remind yourself what is there, say, oh, that's what's in that box, and then lock it right back again."

He threw the pretend key from the balcony, and, when a car below crunched over a palm frond, I imagined that it had hit the street. Then he threw the key again, then again.

"Do you see?"

And because I held him responsible for my sadness, at least my immediate sadness—it was his job that had pulled me from my junior year in high school two weeks into the start, he was the one who said sir, yes, sir, I will come, I will pack my family and fly them across the continent, across the ocean, back to the most geographically isolated island on the planet, and I will do it tomorrow—or because he was sitting across from me, the beer forgotten the same way he wanted me to forget my friends, I nodded my head.

"Good job," he said, and stood, glancing down to the street below, maybe for the gathering of keys. He grabbed his beer, opened the sliding screen door to the room. "That's the way."

On the balcony of the Hilton, sun sinking into the ocean, my mother inside making bologna sandwiches once again for dinner because we had no oven, no stove, my father yelling at my brothers to "knock it off" as they jumped from bed to bed because we had no backyard, I locked the box, locked it tight, and vowed not to open it again.

52

The Cowgirl

At the age of twelve, still living in Hawaii, the cowgirl has hair growing under her arms. It can't be sopped up. Toilet paper isn't enough. She tries pulling the individual hairs out, but they slip between her fingers, curl even tighter next to her skin. She imagines telling her mother.

Here her mother is, on her hands and knees, the bottle of Futura at her heels, waxing the floor.

"Don't walk on my floors," her mother says, as she moves her arms in long arcs, a ripple of wax fanning out in front of the yellow sponge.

"I have hair growing under my arms and I don't know what to do," the cowgirl says.

"Fine, just don't walk on my floors."

The cowgirl cannot have this conversation. Long before Heloise and scientific housekeeping, her mother divided their house into four quadrants. Each week she cleaned one quadrant, dusted the baseboards, the blinds, cleared the cobwebs and dust bunnies, so that by the end of the month the entire house had been touched by her hands. And it was her hands, her knees, never a mop. Mops didn't clean well enough. Laundry on Tuesdays and Saturdays, Tuesdays for clothes, and Saturdays for sheets and towels. Dinner every night, four food groups and lit candles. You ate what was on your plate and you did it without complaint. Then she cleaned the kitchen and pulled out the ironing board. How do you casually say to your mother that you are sprouting hair when you can't even see her behind the pile of folded laundry she carries up the stairs?

It takes six or eight months for my mother to realize, why, at the age of twelve, I no longer wear anything sleeveless. She says it has just occurred to her that I have underarm hair, but I will always think that somehow I made a mistake and my secret was found out. Maybe Mrs. Hansen saw the hair when she put me in the shower. Maybe my mother could see the dark mass underneath my white t-shirts.

One afternoon in the middle of my sixth-grade year she enters my bedroom with a small gray box. I sit on the floor, my *Star Wars* cards arranged around me. She glances at the "I Love Mark Hamill" on my wall, the dozens of pictures taped beneath and between the letters. For once, she doesn't say anything about using tape on the walls. Instead, she asks if she can sit beside me on the floor.

What she pulls from the box is a small, round, electric razor, avocado-colored.

"This is the razor I used in college," she says. "It's a good one to start with because it won't cut you."

To get to the electrical outlet, she has to move a pile of dirty clothes. From the stack, she pulls two uniform shirts and tosses them into the hall, then returns to finding the plug.

Cross-legged, she sits beside me in the afternoon sun. Outside my window, the plumeria bobs in the breeze, its long limbs flagged with red flowers. A gecko clicks nearby in the house.

"See," she says, "you just run the razor along your arm like this." She has her shirt halfway off and holds her left arm high in the air. In contrast to her tanned skin, her underarm is white and delicate.

"It doesn't hurt," she adds, and offers the blade to me so that I can feel the vibrations with my fingers. Dark hairs lay trapped in the blade, the plastic dull and marked from years of use.

"You try."

But as I lift my shirt, prepare to bring the razor to my skin, the door to my room bursts open.

"Mom, where are you?!"

Scott stands at the door, his mother and sister on the ground, shirts half off, an avocado razor buzzing the afternoon air. Before he can say anything, the smile already on his face, my mom leaps up and pushes Scott from the room, suggesting a snack and the kitchen. She shuts the door behind me, the razor still vibrating on the floor.

I cannot use the electric razor; I expect my brother to enter the room as soon as I turn the switch. Suspecting this, my mother leaves a package of disposable razors on my bed for me one afternoon when I return from school.

At school, I swelter in the black Members Only jacket that conceals the fact that I don't wear a bra and have no need for one. I wear t-shirts into the ocean over my bathing suit to conceal the hair under my arms. I bury soiled underwear beneath the dirty clothes. I am running out of hiding places. Still, I stuff the razors under the bed. Every few days, I sneak one to the shower in the folds of a towel.

53

The Boy

In the summer before seventh grade, Karen moves into the house next to mine, turning Sandy and me into a threesome. Karen brings a matching bedroom set and an older brother, Paul, who is fifteen.

Though his face is covered in acne and he is fanatical about the Phillies and playing Dungeons and Dragons, I am thrilled by any notice Paul pays me. And because Paul pays attention to me, when the boys at school don't, I encourage him, even as I pretend to dislike him. The confusion feels both dangerous and familiar. At Karen's house for the afternoon and knowing Paul is around, I go to the refrigerator, open the door, and bend over looking for a Coke. He often then appears from his bedroom, having heard the refrigerator seal break, and gooses me on the way to the laundry room. His hand fits easily into the bow of my bottom, fingers almost touching my vagina, sending a shiver through my body.

"Ah!" I say, a weak objection.

Later I return to the kitchen for another Coke, and Paul does as well.

SOMETIMES HE CHASES me around the yard so that he can pin me to the ground with his "Vulcan death grip," sometimes he threatens to pull down the elastic top of my romper, some-times he points his finger up the opening between my thigh and the Dove shorts I wear after school and asks, "What's up there?" And I laugh the whole time, my heart racing not from exertion but from the excitement of not knowing what might come next. Could the Vulcan death grip lead to French kissing? Would I want to kiss him? Would he possibly want to kiss me?

One afternoon when I am in eighth grade, we sit on the curb outside Paul and Karen's house. I have recently purchased my first boom box, a cassette/radio player from the exchange that cost forty-nine dollars. For months I have been saving for it, squirreling away the money I make from my paper route, visiting the radio every time my mom takes me to the store. When we go to the beach on the weekends, I bring the boom box with me, draped in a t-shirt, and set it on my towel as I lay in the sun. The ocean has become a place to cool off, rather than to play in. Now I work on my tan.

The night before, I had made what I thought was a mixtape. Because I didn't know what kind of music I was supposed to like and because I had no patience to listen to the radio waiting for songs I didn't know to play, I simply stuck in a tape and hit record, then left the room. So what I have that afternoon is a thirty-minute recording of 98 Rock, commercials and all. In my good fortune, though, I have taped John Cougar's "Hurt So Good." When it comes on, Paul turns up the volume and grins.

"This is a great song," he says.

I nod my head, paying attention to the chorus so I can find it again.

Karen skates up and down the street in front of us. She is working on her spins and every now and then asks me to watch her. Sometimes she falls as she whirls around, but our thighs are so marked with scabs and cuts from falling that we don't pay any attention to fresh wounds.

Paul sits next to me. I can feel the hair on his legs brush mine. When the song ends, he rewinds the tape and plays it again.

"Jen, you know what hurts so good means, don't you?" he asks, smiling.

I look at him and can tell he is toying with me. His arched eyebrows and narrowed eyes suggest something sexual. His full lips glisten with saliva in the sun. Karen flies past us, the steady swoosh of her skates as she pushes off with each foot.

"Yes," I say, but I have no idea.

"You don't know," he responds, laughing at me. "You're such a virgin."

I can see the whiskers growing on his chin that he hasn't shaved, dark hairs curling around themselves, pimples gathering at the point of his chin and on the flats of his cheeks.

"Whatever," I say.

"In algebra class I sit in the back and make out with my girlfriend Marissa. We mash for the entire period. The teacher doesn't even notice. He just goes on teaching. He's such an idiot."

I try to picture Paul making out with Marissa, a girl I decide right there has wavy hair and a clear complexion, Chiclet teeth, no glasses. And then his teacher, male, gray-haired, at the front of the room solving for "x." I consider how they might hold their bodies in their desks, where they would put their hands, their books. And then I feel a swelling hurt at the thought that Paul has a girlfriend.

"When you make it, it hurts some," he says, "but the hurt is good." He looks at me, and I try to match his gaze, but then drop it. My stomach skitters.

Karen has skated far from us, the hum of her skates in the background. I have never realized how green his eyes are.

"Whatever," I say again and look across the street from us into the empty yard. A car drives past, mynahs leaping from the asphalt into the limbs of the nearby mango. As I sit on the curb, I trace my fingers along the patchwork of scabs on my outer thigh, feel the sting when I catch the healing edge, imagine the blood coming to the surface, seeping into the sun, then return to pull the scab again, feel the bright pain again, Paul's green eyes, his lips, the way the hair on his legs brushes against mine, ball bearings in the distance, Karen twirling around and around.

54

The Lunch

One afternoon my father takes me out for lunch to the Pearl City Tavern, a bar/restaurant a few miles from Pearl Harbor. It's not my birthday, not the end of the school year, but it feels like some kind of celebration. Having never been out to lunch with just my father, I am nervous and excited. Walking across the parking lot and toward the restaurant, he puts his arm around my waist and shows me how to hook my fingers in his belt loops to stay attached. I feel very adult, walking this way, somehow longer in body.

The tavern is gloomy. Businessmen dressed in Aloha shirts and hunched over plates of meatloaf and teriyaki fill the booths. The waitress shows us to a table, and I sit down across from my father. When he orders a Coke for me, it comes with a yellow and red umbrella floating on the ice, some of the only bits of color in the room. I run the toothpick between finger and thumb, twirling the umbrella like a top, watching the colors blur and meld. Later, at home, I will open and close it until the balsawood ribs finally break, puncturing the yellow paper.

There is something mildly illicit about the Pearl City Tavern. Perhaps it is the darkness, the light bulbs concealed by thick slabs of orange and red glass and emitting a watery glow; perhaps it is the waitresses who are dressed in short

skirts and whose faces are as worn as the leather in the
booths; perhaps it is only the projections of a twelve-year-
old girl with a bright imagination who is used to eating at
McDonald's and is overwhelmed by a menu so tall that it
bends in half when she opens it. Whatever the reason, in the
warm, damp darkness of the restaurant, sitting in a booth
across from my father, my feet unable to touch the ground,
I worry that those around me are gamblers or drug dealers
or unfaithful husbands, that my father and I eat among dis-
honest men. I might be seen as one of them.

That is, until the fashion show starts, shattering the business of men eating. Surprised, we turn our heads in the direction of a stage that stretches like a hide across the front of
the restaurant. Even with the overhead lights turned up, I
am unprepared for the carnival of color that enters with the
women: reds, blues, and screaming yellows. The models move
about the room, in between the tables and booths, dressed
in outfits sold at stores in the mall. Dangling from sleeves
and hems, price tags flitter after them, hurrying to catch up.

I cannot imagine why there was a fashion show in a
mall restaurant in the middle of the day for an audience of
bankers, insurance salesmen, and a father and his daughter.
My memory feels murky like the lighting. But I find it must
happen this way. I need to be in a body teetering on the
edge of adolescence, and my father must take me to lunch.
When he does, the world will crack open in a sea of fabric
and light this moment when I am chosen.

55

The Sleepover

Days after the John Cougar discussion, I spend the night at Karen's house. Both our parents are out for the night, attending the navy's Birthday Ball. Earlier in the evening, my mother had put on bright coral lipstick that matched the polish on her toes. In strappy heels and a long dress, she looked taller than her five-foot-three. The day at the beach had given her brown skin a deep glow. "Don't stay up too late," she said before kissing me good night, her Blue Grass perfume swallowing the two of us in a field of scent. "We have church in the morning."

Karen, Paul, and I watch TV for a while. *Fantasy Island* is on, and we want to see who is guest starring. The Mitchells use their screened-in porch as a family room just as we do, so as we sit in front of the TV we listen to the night sounds that chorus just beyond the lanai.

"Junk," Karen says, when we see it's a rerun. "It's not even a good one."

Paul and I say nothing, though I look at him to see if he concurs. He lies stretched out on the couch, the hair of his belly peeking out from beneath the cut-off shirt he wears. It is the dark hair of a man, not a boy.

Karen and I sit on chairs across the room. I hold my empty ice cream bowl in my lap.

"I'm going to bed," Karen announces and then looks to me. I stand when she does, follow her from the room.

"I'm staying up," Paul says, and I know he is saying this to me, can feel his eyes on my back. I don't need to turn to see the blue tones of the television bouncing off his cheeks and forehead.

Karen falls asleep quickly, and I lie next to her in the bed, thinking about Paul in the other room. At one point the volume seems to get louder, and I think of it as an invitation. Before I leave Karen's room, I put my shorts back on and rake my fingers through my hair.

Paul is still draped on the couch where I left him, M*A*S*H on the television now. He pats the space in front of him. Without a word, I slide my body in front of his. Outside, date palms clack in the gentle wind.

Klinger wanders across the screen with a pink stole flirting with his knees. He wears a flowered-print dress and carries his gun; chandelier earrings brush his shoulders. Paul shifts his weight, at the same time bringing his fingers to my leg. At first, his hand just rests on my knee. We both stare at the television, neither acknowledging the shift. Nor is anything said when he brings his fingers up my leg, tracing my lower thigh. I have been shaving my legs for over a year, and I can feel how easily his fingers glide the surface of my skin. His touch is gentle, quiet; my heart beats madly beneath my shirt.

M*A*S*H goes to commercial and Paul takes the cue to move higher on my leg, now circling my thigh, sometimes retreating down to the lower parts of my leg only to return and move even higher. I shift, move my legs, and he stops, then begins again, ankle, to calf, to knee, to thigh.

I feel his breathing, gentle like his touch. The TV blurs before me, and I close my eyes, crickets, cars outside, a cat leaping from the wall around the lanai.

When he gets to the top of my thigh, he moves his hand slowly under my shorts. His fingers flirt with the elastic of my underwear, push gently underneath. I shift again, he begins again, only this time starting at my thigh. When his hand moves beneath my underwear again, deeper this time, maybe touching the hair that grows coarse like the hair on his belly, I jump up.

He rises to sitting on the couch, looks at me in the dark, his eyes eager but kind.

"I can't," I say and run from the room, unsure of what I can't do.

In the bed next to Karen, her breath deep in sleep, the sheet warm from her body, I try to catch my racing heart. First shame, followed by anger, at myself and then at Paul because that is easier. I blame him that I don't understand the edges of my own desire.

56

The Fish

Not long before we return to Virginia for a second tour of
duty at the Pentagon, my father charters a boat at Pearl Harbor
and insists we all go deep-sea fishing. He must sense the
fracturing on the horizon and sees a boat—all of us together
and miles from shore—as a way to forestall the scattering.
Or maybe he wants to float one last time on the sea, a body
not unlike the grasslands of Nebraska, wide and open and
undulating eternally under the same strong sun. But driving
to the harbor that morning in the still-dark feels symbolic;
it feels like something needs to happen here that we can
carry with us to Virginia, back to the same brick house with
a swimming pool in the backyard.

It is still dark outside when the boat pulls away from the
dock at Pearl Harbor, though the darkness of first light, a
shallow darkness really, grainy like an old movie. We motor
quietly past the sleeping frigates and destroyers, their
sides rising in steep walls from the harbor, decks and guns
indiscernible above us, but there. A few sailors, returning
from leave in Waikiki or the CPO club, nod and wave as our
fishing boat passes. Having checked in with the officer on
deck, they move up the gangplank and disappear into the
vast belly of the ship. We pass the empty dry dock and the

submarine base where boats float like slugs, trailing oil along the surface of the water in ribbons of slime.

Motoring up the channel, I am surrounded by the familiars of my world. At the age of fourteen, the ships and boats are, for me, what trees and ditches must be for other kids. Many of the subs I can identify, like dolls, by name, and those I cannot, I know by class. A few—the *Indy*, the *Tunny*, the *Aspro*—are familiar both inside and out. I have washed my face in the tiny metal sink that crowds the far corner of the state room, run my hands along the ladder rails, rifled through the video collections, and slid the narrow halls as the submarine dives and surfaces, demonstrating its prowess to the dependents during cruises. Among my prized possessions is a picture of me aboard one of the subs, signed by the captain, proof that I am a part of this world.

At the back of the boat from where the fishing lines will eventually be reeled out, I sit and watch the subs grow smaller and smaller as we continue to push up the channel. Unlike those times I have stood with my friends to welcome their fathers home from sea or to see them off, this time I am the one leaving the shore. The boats lay bow to stern in sleeping rows along the dock. Soon only the outlines of their sails can be seen, creating rows of skinny crosses in the growing light, hugging the waters at the mouth of the harbor.

Before long, the Dramamine starts working and I fall asleep on the plastic red cushions that double as life preservers. They are faded by the sea air, smell of salt, and look as if they couldn't save themselves let alone my eighty-pound body. But they make a decent pillow, the stiff fabric growing warm in the morning sun.

Having found the freedom of open water and no longer wedded to posted speed limits and the restriction on wakes, the fishing boat turns straight into the waves, heading for the deep sea. I know from my father that "deep sea" is geographically defined and is an almost lawless space where the rules of engagement slacken and a nation's legal jurisdiction ends. In my mind it is a wild place, the wilderness heart of the ocean where pirates and outlaws commandeer unprotected boats, and ships disappear without a trace. Uncivilized and raw, it is also where the tuna and the *mahi mahi* live, and we are hours from it, so I gladly yield to the drug.

Lapping at the edges of my mind as I drift off to sleep is the thought that a submarine may silently swim beneath us; its bullet-shaped body moving through the water, darting in and out of the coral reefs like a giant fish.

BY MID-MORNING WE are deep into the ocean. Birds no longer follow our boat, having decided we have no bait to lose. With nothing in sight except the black water welling and rolling beneath us, the boat doesn't feel isolated as much as framed, the horizon carefully cutting a box in which we troll around. I eat saltines made saltier by the air. My mother has packed a lunch of peanut butter sandwiches, but like everything else on the boat they smell of fish. Too excited by the imminent release of the fishing lines, my brothers, now aged seven and ten, refuse to eat. I am too seasick.

The captain begins untangling a mass of huge plastic lures in bright pinks and jellied purples. Spangles and glittered fringe work to conceal the deadly four-pronged hooks, but they are there. As the captain knots the squid-like lures onto the end of two-hundred-pound test line, I wonder from my prone position what fish would be desperate enough to eat something as unnatural as jellied neon.

"What will we catch?" I ask the captain, after he has sent out six lines—four off the stern and two from rods placed high and off to the side of the boat. With the release of the lines, the birds return, seemingly crazed with the possibility of food. They cartwheel behind the boat, diving to the water and back into the sky, shrieking like ghosts or mothers who have lost their children. They are everywhere and all at once.

"Dolphin," he replies.

I know he doesn't mean Flipper and am proud in my knowledge, hoping the captain notices that this sleepy girl is also a smart one. Dolphin are also large fish, *mahi mahi* in Hawaiian. They, not porpoise, are the symbol for the naval submarine fleet. When a sailor becomes a submariner, he earns his dolphins—recognition that he, too, now has the right to swim below. What appears initially empty, landless stretches of water interrupted only by wave, is actually quite full, full of bodies, of subs, of sailors, of fish.

Bored with waiting for the first strike of the day, I peer over the side of the boat as we troll around in sweeping circles. Water splashes me and I think of sliding smoothly into the sea, joining the dolphin and tuna. How deep the water must be here, deep enough to conceal entire mountain ranges, canyons, channels, and trenches. Deep enough to conceal the Pacific Fleet's submarines.

An order is established for reeling in the fish. I will be third, after Scott and Bryan, and my parents will follow us. I bring my head up long enough to hear my place in line.

The tuna begin striking around noon. Yellow-finned *ahi*. Scott and Bryan run to their stations, hefting the giant rods and with help from the captain positioning them in the silver cups that sit between their legs in the fighting chairs.

"It's all in the back," my father yells. "Use your back. Wear out the fish. Remember it's not just strength. Never strength. Stamina."

They shriek in laughter. It is fun. Bracing themselves against the side of the boat, straining and laughing, they reel in the line, sun glinting off their blonde heads, flashing and brilliant.

"Great! Great! You're doing great!"

I stand back, under the awning and out of the sun. After a long struggle, my brothers land their fish almost simultaneously. Gray, bullet-shaped, twenty-pound Ahi hit the boat deck with a thunk. The fish thrash and twist, sides heaving with the effort. Their colors drain immediately, returning with the salt water back into the sea. Where is the yellow of the fin, I wonder. Into the ice chest with the sandwiches they go. Birds move in closer, threatening.

Hours pass. We land close to forty tuna, both yellow fin and Aku, their dark-meated cousins. The ice chest is full with their bodies, overfull, tails and fins bursting beneath the lid. Every now and then the cooler lid shudders with the effort of a not-yet-dead fish trying to regain the water. The ice prolongs the freshness of their meat but not their lives.

"How will we ever eat all this?!" my mom laughs.

I realize only then that the fish are coming home with us. They will fill the back of our van, the floor between the seats, the freezer. Salt water will remain in their bodies like a memory only to dribble out when they are cleaned. We will label the paper packages in black marker, seal them with masking tape, and store them with the ice cream in the deep freeze. Later my mom will shape their bodies into quenelles or sauté filets and serve them to guests for dinner. And I will eat them.

At some point I, too, reel a fish in. I am sure I do. I remember the feel of the acrylic rod, my dad's hand on my shoulder, the on-and-off pull of the fish against me. Mostly the on-and-off pull. Then surrender. Then another flat gray fish. I return to my spot out of the sun while the rest reel fish after fish onto the deck. The Hawaiian sun or the lack of food or the Dramamine has made me dizzy. I try to remember which of the fish flopping on the deck is mine, but they all look the same.

It is getting late.

57

The Curb

Karen and Paul's family are relocating to the East Coast as well. They will be in Virginia Beach; we'll be in Fairfax. Days before he leaves the island, Paul spends the night at our house. The rest of his family has gone to another island, and he is staying home to take a practice PSAT. Throughout dinner he brushes my bare leg under the table while my father tells Scott how to build his tree fort. Each time his skin touches mine, I stop eating, my fork halfway to my mouth.

Days before, Paul and I had taken the bus downtown to see *Clash of the Titans*. I considered it a date even though Karen was with us. Since the conversation on the curb, he hadn't mentioned Marissa, and my anger from the night he traced my thigh dissolved with the daylight.

During the movie, we shared popcorn from the same tub, our hands reaching in, fingers slick with butter, touching. I tried to time my bites to align with his so that our hands would be reaching for the next handful at the same time. Around us couples sat holding hands, the girls hiding their heads in their boyfriends' chests as the battles unfolded on the screen. I made sure my leg touched Paul's, but he never ran his fingers along my skin.

After dinner we sit on the curb, ants crawling along our feet, the sunset turning the sky an electric orange. No one else is on the streets and for once the trade winds aren't blowing. The air is thick and hot.

Paul rubs the thin skin above my ankle, at first squashing an ant and then just remaining. For a long time, we don't talk.

"Are you worried about the test tomorrow?" I ask him.

He shakes his head, brown hair falling in his face.

"What about moving?"

He shakes his head again. I expect him to say something about how he is going to ace the test or find a real girlfriend in Virginia, but instead he turns to me and reaches for the gold-dipped maile leaf pendant on my necklace.

"What's this?" he asks.

I tell him how Karen and I had found the necklace at the swap meet, how we had had to search through all the pokololo leaves to find a maile. I assume he will say something about smoking dope or how I should have chosen the pot leaf, but he just keeps fingering the necklace.

He has to sit at an awkward angle to reach the necklace, so I turn to face him. He moves the charm up and down the S-link chain and I feel the vibrations of the charm as it clicks along.

A car drives past, and we both turn to face forward again. Mr. Willard from down the street waves to us and we wave back.

"Kevin is such a dork," I offer, thinking of the Willard boys, two pasty teenagers who look identical.

We turn back toward one another as Mr. Willard makes his way down the street. But this time Paul runs his fingers along my collarbone as he pulls the leaf back and forth. Then he stops and follows some invisible line down my breastbone and into my blouse.

My skin is warm from where he touches me. His fingers stop at the top button of my blouse, halted.

Paul looks at me, index finger hooked around the button of my blouse, and I realize he could kiss me, want him to kiss me.

I must be pulling away, though, because the next thing he says is "Come here. I won't bite."

I inch back toward him, our knees touching. I can still feel the place on my breastbone where his fingers have been, and I want to feel them there again.

Then he leans his body close to mine, really close this time, pulling me toward him. His green eyes are open, as are his lips, lips that look soft and warm like his fingers.

In a few weeks his family will be moving to Virginia Beach. We will follow. I know already that I will miss him, miss his attention, miss the way he tickles my neck when no one else is looking. At the same time, I don't want him to kiss me because I am unsure of what would happen next, when the kiss wasn't good, and he laughed or teased or simply turned his back.

So I break away, as I did the night in front of the television, only this time without any excuse, and I run from him, as well as from the enlisted men who whistle at me when I walk from the exchange, and the puddle of urine on the concrete floor of the Quonset hut, and the blue veins on my Grandpa's hands, and the stranger at the mall who traps me in the cosmetics aisle and spits profanity into my ears. I run from them all.

58

The Deep

Dedicated to all submariners who lost their lives on duty, Subase Chapel sits on a quiet corner of the Pearl Harbor Naval Base. Each of the stained-glass windows contains tiny submarines among the brightly colored pieces. You have to hunt for the black subs, though; they lurk, as in real life, at the edges. In the back of the church, hanging in the stairwell leading up to the balcony, is a giant picture of a golden Jesus hovering over a submarine, rays of light lifting the boat to heaven. The picture is entitled "Our Lord of the Deep," and I was always scared of it. Jesus never looked happy and the oranges and yellows made me worry for the safety of the boat.

Each Sunday we would pray for those under the sea. And each Sunday I would envision Mr. Hansen when we sang the "Submariner's Hymn." Loud and clear I would begin, "Eternal Father, Strong to Save/ Whose arm hath bound the restless wave/ Who bidd'st the mighty ocean deep/ Protect each one we ask of Thee." At these moments, encouraged by the voices joining mine and the welling of the music, I pictured the *Tunny* imploding from pressure, crashing against a reef, sinking into blackness, or taking enemy fire. I had seen the movies. I had watched the soldiers and sailors on base as they practiced for war, running in platoons with guns at the

ready, humping their loads past the golf course and commissary, their bodies moving in unison like so many fish.

Subase Chapel sat twenty yards away from a giant tower
that dominated Pearl Harbor. I could see it from almost anywhere on base. Red-and-white striped like an enormous pep-
permint stick, the tower was a training site for submariners
and was full of seawater. As their final stage in earning their
dolphins, men had to enter at the bottom of the tower, pass
through a chamber, and then swim the hundred feet to the
top. It was an exercise meant to demonstrate their preparation for escaping from a crippled sub. Along the way were
oxygen tanks if a sailor panicked and needed air. After all,
they were not fish. Real submariners, though, made it the
first time, in one breath, shooting through fathoms of water
to a second surface, having left the initial one behind. The
gasp of air, securing their dolphins, the triumph of disci-
pline over nature, over the body, the tower was a symbol of
strength and hardship and sacrifice. I knew the risks those
in the military undertook. And I sang for them every Sunday
because I knew that the real ocean was so much deeper than
that tower.

59

The Fall

"Don't slam the door," my mother calls from the kitchen.

I stand in the family room, out of breath, the TV on but no one watching.

"Where's Dad?" I ask. I realize when I see no one in the family room that I have run up the sidewalk looking for someone in particular.

"In the carport working on the van. Where's Paul? Are you two coming inside? It's time for bed. He has that test tomorrow."

"Yeah." I exit the back door to the carport, making sure that Paul can't see me. Now that the sun has set, the evening is dark. I find my father squatting at the rear of the van, the engine flap open, a bright light clamped to a nearby pole and shining a spotlight on my father's balding head.

His hands are covered in grease as are his brown coveralls. But he is humming, which indicates that the job has been going well.

"Hey, Dad," I say, dropping to the grass near him, conscious that my voice quivers. "What are you working on?"

"Changing spark plugs," he responds, but he is clearly surprised that I have come to sit by him because he stops, ratchet in hand, and looks at me. "What's wrong?"

"Nothing," I say. But I start to cry.

He stands and wipes his greasy hands on the red towel he pulls from a pocket. His arm brushes the lamp clamped to the pole and light shivers against cement and grass.

"Then why are you crying?"

"It's nothing, Dad."

But I rarely come to my father for reassurance. My mother is the one who makes my world okay after my father has yelled or I've gotten a C on a test or my braces have to stay on for another six months. When I cry in front of my father, it is in anger or exasperation, not because a boy bewilders and confuses.

"Must be something."

I have his attention. "Nothing. Paul did something, that's all," I say, but I know it is enough.

"What did he do?" he asks, his voice bristling. He stops wiping his hands.

"Nothing."

"Did he touch you?"

"Not really."

And that is all it takes, just as I know it will. By the time I get to the house, having chased my father up the lawn, he is yelling at Paul.

"You are a guest in my house," I hear him bellow. "When you are in my house you do what I say."

"Yes, sir."

"Don't touch my daughter. Don't even talk to her."

I stay outside, too mortified at my own actions to witness the fallout. Without the sun, the birds have returned to their trees, leaving the night empty, not unlike a house after the movers have packed us out, the rooms echoing voices and footsteps, the familiar grown hollow and cold. I stand under the plumeria, the white flowers above me but invisible in

the dark. I am not the girl pushed into the bushes by two
older boys, underwear at her ankles, waiting for her father
to save her. I am the boys themselves, a bully, a coward, a
girl who calls her father because she knows he will come. I
have manipulated my father in the same way I manipulated
Paul, but at the time I could not have said why. I could not
have articulated the pleasure I took in my power. The military might make me relocate, my father might explode over
the price of gasoline, the Soviets might press the red button
first, but I could get Paul into trouble.

That night I hear Paul crying in the room across the hall
from mine. I want to go to him and apologize, but I can't
imagine what I would say. Instead, I stay in bed and finger
the gold-dipped *maile*. I run the charm along the S-chain
link, creating a scattershot of sound.

60

The Fish

We are headed in when the marlin strikes. The captain has pulled in all lines but one. The strike is solid and the reel whizzes as more and more line is released. After he cuts the engine, the captain runs to the back of the boat, yelling and screaming about the great sporting fish.

It is my mom's turn in line, and the captain straps her in, the thick rod in the cup between her legs.

My dad paces behind her, excited by the prospect of landing a giant fish. I stay under the awning where I have spent most of the day, ceding the majority of the deck to my brothers who are sunburned but happy.

"Cynde, pull on the rod. Are you sure you set the hook? You still have him, right?"

My father edges closer to my mother, puts his hand on the rod, pulls back with her.

"I'm trying," she says.

"No, not like that. You're moving sideways. You need to reel straight on."

My mother adjusts her body in the chair, tries to mimic the actions my father makes in the air.

"You're going to lose him, Cynde. You're going to lose him."

"I'm trying," my mom says again, and as evidence of her exertion I can see the sweat gathering under her arms, dampening the fabric on her cotton shirt.

My father leans into my mother, his knee perched on the edge of the fighting chair, both hands on the rod.

"I'll swing the boat around," the captain says, removing himself from the scene and leaving only my family at the back of the boat. The marlin bends the pole at such an angle it will surely snap.

"You're going to lose him!" my father says again, only now he seems panicked by the loss, as if losing this fish means losing something else, something much bigger. He pushes at my mother with his hip, bumps against her several times, and then, like a blown seed, she simply lifts from the chair and my father takes her place. Behind him the four of us gather, no one saying a word.

FOR WHAT SEEMS like hours but is really minutes, my dad reels and releases, listening for cues from the captain who has returned from the helm and now paces the length of the deck where my father once strode. As my dad throws his body back and forth in the fighting chair, my brothers hoot and holler, laughing at the possibility of this great fish. Confusion grows around us with each length of line my father purchases. The only other crew member joins the captain and our six bodies no longer seem to fit on the boat. Yells from the captain collide with the shrieking gulls, tearing the air in two. Beneath the commotion, steady like the breath, the reel wheezes as line is given and reclaimed, given and reclaimed. The eighty-pound marlin fights with all it has.

When the marlin breaks the surface for the first time none of us is prepared. Spiraling up from the water, he hangs for minutes in the air, his sleek black body pressed onto the background of sky like a gallery painting. His long nose points

up, out, and beyond. Without a splash, he plunges back into
the ocean, a perfect dive.

The boat falls silent.

MY DAD CONTINUES to struggle—though he's tiring—reeling
and releasing, reeling and releasing. Each time the marlin
breaks the surface, arcing in the air and cutting back into
the water, my dad stops. In fact, each time the marlin bursts
forth, erupting like a submarine in an emergency blow, we
all stare.

Such magnificence. Like a ballerina holding the air, the
earth's forces seem to have no effect on its body. What the
marlin is really doing, I soon realize, is fighting.

We first see the shimmering colors and giant sail when
my dad brings him close to the boat. My mother, brothers,
and I move to the railing so we can see the marlin as he is
caught. Even through the froth of water, its iridescent sides,
rippling flashes of blues, greens, and reds are visible. The
captain helps guide the line, keeping the marlin close. He
yells to the four of us to move out of the way, clearing the
back of the boat. Pinned to the side of the boat but still in
the water, the marlin's long, straight nose spears the air, its
length in proportion to his six-foot body; the sail, running
the stretch of his spine, flaps up and down, convulses. The
pale pink of his belly stands in stark contrast to the oil black
of his back.

By the time we pull him (hands, nets, hooks), his colors
have already begun to fade. Salt water and blood spill over
the sides. Spasms. He barely fits, this giant fish. He barely
fits on the deck. His tail is bent up the side of the boat and
we have to move the cooler so that his head can rest on the

floor. I look into his large, flat eye, and wonder what he has seen under the sea.

Then the captain bludgeons him with a thick club that has been conjured from the air. He pounds and pounds on the fish's body, mostly at the head and eye but also the sides and heart. The marlin does not have time to gasp or flop before the club falls on him again. Bloody scales fly off his body and stick to my legs and arms. Pieces of marlin, translucent, uncolored, visible only because of the blood, spatter my shins, the boat, the club, my brothers. Rivers of blood mix with the deck water and rush back into the sea, red lines running down the sides of the boat. His eye is fractured and fills with blood. All color save red are gone from his skin. Like a fish at market, he looks cold, dead. Moments ago he was dancing, and now, because he is too big for the cooler, he is crammed into a semicircle on our fishing boat deck. There is no longer any room to move.

I want to say that no one speaks the entire trip back to the harbor. I want to say that we stand in mute witness to the death of this fish, realizing it is the very least we can do. I want to say that this is the moment I begin to understand that the peace we experience in the United States is one secured by force. I want to say that I watch my childhood drain with the blood from the deck. But none of that would be true. On the way back to the harbor, my father apologizes repeatedly to my mother for catching her fish, while I sleep on the boat cushions, and Scott and Bryan count the number of fish we have taken from the sea.

61

The Wrench

We return to Virginia and the Pentagon in 1983, back to the same brick house my parents bought in 1975 with the falling acorns and the cold mornings where the driveway becomes a sheet of ice. It is the year Reagan will launch Star Wars, and the year I will begin high school at Oakton, student population four thousand, where I will sit with red-haired Rosie at the cafeteria table reading books and eating homemade lunches without uttering a single word.

At the age of fourteen, I enter a depression that parallels the oncoming winter, feel darkness inside me, contemplate suicide in abstract terms. No sun, no friends, a father who demands that I anticipate the next tool he will need, I beg my mother to buy me my first pair of contact lenses before I begin the school year. They don't arrive in time and on the first day of high school I wear my Navy Exchange glasses, cuffed purple corduroys two sizes too large, and an acrylic argyle sweater with diamonds down the front. In the sea of students, no one even notices.

This time around, my room is in the basement, leaving the upstairs bedrooms to my parents and brothers. Because we have lived in military quarters or rental houses for so long, I am excited to have a room of my own and paint it the color I have long thought a room should be painted—pink with white trim, the colors a six-year-old might choose. If my parents could have afforded it, I would have asked for a gold-trimmed canopy bed. The pink isn't enough to lift my spirits; almost immediately I sense that no other fourteen-year-old would choose such a palette. I sit on my bed, sick in my stomach.

In the basement, I don't fear monsters as much as I do nuclear annihilation. Only a few months ago, I stood aboard a submarine while it shot water slugs from its torpedo tubes, the reverberations felt in my bones. America's nuclear arsenal is not an abstraction for me. At the dinner table we discuss the nuclear threat, and on my own I read about nuclear winter, fall out, and radiation sickness. In my Pepto-Bismol bed-room, I await the event that will leave me dead or alone on the ravaged planet or so poisoned with radiation that I will be confined to a cement-block room for the rest of my life.

Sitting on my bed, I open the same Holly Hobbie diary and write. Upstairs, footfalls land followed by the flush of the toilet. Below, in my bedroom, the windows open to dirt. Very little, except meals, can draw me upstairs. I nurse my anger and isolation, blame my father for the move. In my diary I write:

> Life is hard right now. I have no friends. I miss my old ones. I probably can't get contact lenses and I feel very low at times. I enjoy talking to God and should do it more. I think there may be a nuclear war which we will deserve because the world is falling apart.

At school we do not run air drills or practice finding shelter because we know that nothing would survive nuclear winter. I watch *War Games*, *Top Gun*, and *Red Dawn*, movies that terrify me and teach me to seek comfort in weapons and artillery, in a military that flies the fastest, shoots the farthest, and is not afraid to use its weapons. I have long operated from a position of defensiveness, sure that I will be rejected by everyone. Nuclear deterrence comes as second nature.

And because I have nowhere else to go after school and on the weekends, no kids my own age on the block, no warm nights underneath the thin Hawaiian sky watching the ants climb my shins, I work with my father on the house, the cars, and the yard.

"CRESCENT WRENCH," HE says from beneath the car one night not long after school had begun. His hand shoots out, palm up, waiting for the tool like a surgeon awaits a scalpel.

I peer into the red toolbox and consider the various sizes, all of them silver and cold, grease covering the wheel where you adjust the bite. Large seems best, always can be made smaller. I put the wrench in his hand and wait.

That day at school, I had sat in algebra watching a cheerleader cuff and uncuff her white socks. The girl's ankles were slender, legs like drift wood, with curves and dips and secret places. As she arranged her socks, ran her hands along her smooth shin, she laughed, maybe at the boy behind her or beside her or the one in front of her who had turned around in his seat so that he could see her blonde hair fall in sheaves to her shoulders.

There must be a football game tonight, I thought, or otherwise the cheerleader wouldn't be wearing her uniform, the dark maroon skirt, so short, so startling against the white of her thigh. I wouldn't be going to the game, wouldn't have anyone to go with, wouldn't have known how to find it, what to wear, or any of the cheers this cheerleader yelled out. It didn't matter. I didn't want to go to the game; nor did I want to be swarmed by boys wearing pastel polo shirts turned up at the collar. What I did want, though, was the cheerleader's tiny waist, the way she could perch on the very edge of her chair, almost like she wasn't even there.

"I'm working in a small space, Jennifer. I need something smaller. Get me something smaller."

"I forgot," I say, reaching for the toolbox.

"Think about it. Think where I am."

I rummage through the tools, slender screwdrivers and hammers getting in the way of the wrenches.

"Anticipate! Anticipate!" he yells from beneath the car.

He smacks his right foot, the only part of his body I can see, on the concrete several times before dropping his bent knee to the ground in defeat.

From a tangle of tools, I find a smaller wrench and place it in his outstretched palm. I wait to hear him yell again, try to imagine what the next tool might be so that I can have it ready. I grab both a hammer and the socket set and return to my spot on the cold concrete. Every now and then I hear the grunts my father makes as he tries to loosen the bolt. I try to anticipate it all.

62

The Cowgirl

When we went shopping for back-to-school clothes, my mother had insisted I leave the relative safety of the dressing room to model each new outfit. The store's lights exposed every part of my body. I imagined the other shoppers halting their search through the sale racks to tally the ways in which I looked ridiculous. Although I now realize no one even looked my way, at the time my list of inadequacies assumed pages.

Each of us could have one new set of clothes, no more, my mother had said to me and my brothers as we entered Bradlees. She didn't have to tell us it was all we could afford. Scott and Bryan had groaned about trying on clothes, but soon they each had a new pair of jeans and a long-sleeved shirt. My mother had sent them to watch television on the rows of TVs for sale at the back, while she and I stood beneath the fluorescent lighting, the doors to the fitting rooms worn and dinged.

"Those are okay," my mother said. "How about those?" She pointed to the black polyester pants that ballooned around my knees.

I had no idea. For five years I had worn a school uniform every day. What did kids in Virginia wear to school? Panic climbed my throat.

"They seem big," was all I could muster, because they did. The waist settled at my hips and the cuffs folded like an accordion at the floor.

"Well," my mother said, "You keep getting bigger and I don't know if you're going to stop. We can't keep buying more clothes."

"Okay," I said, because I didn't know if I was going to keep getting bigger either and, while I didn't know what the other kids would be wearing, I did know they wouldn't be splitting their pants at the seams.

63

The Wrench

The wrench is hurled across the concrete slab, knocking
the saw table and spinning in circles before coming to rest
against the orange extension cord.

"Not that one. I need light, no, a hand. Hold this bolt."

I lie down on the cold cement and wedge my body under
the car next to his. The engine sits inches away from his nose,
grey and muddy pans, pipes, and bolts, the axle, the exhaust,
parts I can't possibly name. Dark and tight beneath the car,
my father's face is smudged in grease, long marks under his
eyes, the backs of his hands red from scrapes.

"Can you hold this?"

I try. The wrench feels awkward in my hand, heavier than
it should be.

"Like this, not like that." He presses down on my hand but
not before bumping his elbow into my cheek. "Now hold it."

I falter, and he brings his hand to mine again, harder.
"Hold it."

When I wipe my cheek where the skin still smarts, I feel
the grease mark my fingers leave behind.

"Are you still holding it?"

"Yes."

He begins to push hard against the wrench, working to
free the bolt. Using the back of his hand like a hammer, he

beats against the end of the wrench. It must hurt; I can hear the thump of flesh hitting the metal.

"Hold it," he says between bangs, his head held up off the ground with visible effort. I can see the sweat even in the half-lit darkness. He bangs some more, harder, and I fight to hold my own wrench.

"Use your body," he says, "your weight."

His hand slips, wrist glances the wrench. "Damn it to hell!"

With both hands, I hold my wrench, try to ignore the smell of oil and gasoline, the engine looming above me.

"God bless it! Come on. Don't do this to me. Don't do this!" He is cursing the bolt. I know this. But it feels close.

"I NEED A light. Get the flashlight."

I drop the wrench and use my legs to pull myself out from under the car. Even though the night is dark around me, it feels less dark than beneath the engine. The outdoor lights are on and moths dash their bodies against the white brightness. Closer to the car, my father has clamped two work lights. Beyond these circles, though, the night gathers close and empty. The flashlight, too, is covered in grease, the same way I am now. Thumbprints, handprints, places where the grease streaks in long lines.

I hold my breath when I go under the car the second time, think of snorkeling above the trench near Haliewa, the way the ocean turns black at eighty feet.

"Shine it here." Little room to hold the light. My elbow brushes the ground, scraping the skin.

"No, here. Here! Where I am looking, not where you think I should be looking. Here." And he bangs the fat wrench against the engine, making it ring in my ears, my ears, my ears.

64

The Cards

We are gathered around the wicker table in the basement; the fire has gone out, leaving cold ash and embers that barely flicker. Scott and I play Pitch with my parents, while Bryan maneuvers his Tonka trucks around the family room floor. My father once again explains the rules to the game he has grown up playing, the one that he and his father and brothers and sisters-in-law will play into the early morning while drinking cup after cup of black coffee in the moss-colored mugs my grandma favors. For someone whose knowledge of card games only extends to Hearts and Solitaire, Pitch presents many challenges—pointers versus takers, calling trump, keeping the deuce, bidding your hand, counting cards. I have trouble following, and my father grows more and more impatient with each hand.

"Concentrate," he says, "count the trump."

The wood paneling makes the downstairs feel especially dark, even after we have installed the sliding glass door. We spend most evenings here, though, my mother ironing while Scott and I watch *Love Boat* reruns. The wicker table sits only feet from where I fell from the sofa. When we returned to the house this time, I lifted an edge of the shag rug, hoping to find, maybe, an explanation for the gap that opened in my life when I was seven. Instead, I found blue-foam padding and then a gray concrete slab no different than the one in the garage.

"How many are there again?" I ask. "How do I know?" So many hands have already been played, trump uncounted, takers, points. My partner, my father, has already gotten angry because I didn't "play my hand."

"Thirteen. It's simple. Just count."

Like waves, I think.

Scott has made his cards into a fan and is tapping Bryan on the head with them. My mother sits next to me but stares out the sliding glass door, past the reflection of this scene, and into the darkness, the woods, the place where our yard ends. She is thinking of what she has to do that night after we are in bed, or how to make the curtains in the living room last another year, or whether there is enough milk in the refrigerator for breakfast. Or maybe she is remembering hoisting her son from the chlorine or taping God's eyes to hospital walls, or maybe nothing at all, a song in her head, "A Bicycle Built for Two." Her hand holds the edge of the next card she will play because she knows the game so well that the hands are played before they have begun.

"Think it through. Stop putting up mental blocks. Just think!" My father bangs the glass on the table, on accident perhaps, and causes my mother to jump.

Bryan knocks Scott's hand away and the cards go flying.

"I'm not."

"You are. You're choosing not to understand." He looks me in the eye when he says this, his own eyes full of blame and incomprehension.

"I'm not."

"The ten, the ten, you play the ten."

When he and I "go set" because I have not covered his three, he slams the cards to the table. "Diamonds are clumping. No one is shuffling right." He begins to madly swirl the cards around on the glass table, trying to get them shuffled in a way that will produce a more satisfactory ending. When he discovers that Scott hasn't retrieved all the cards off the floor, he mutters "God bless it" and reshuffles again.

"This game is easy. You just have to learn to think."

AFTER I LEAVE the table in tears, I imagine my mother gathers the cards and carefully folds the score sheet in two. The pencil, she notices, needs to be sharpened. Grabbing a deck without the jokers, my father sets up for solitaire in the quiet, his angry breaths slowly calming as he finds his aces. Scott and Bryan are both on the floor. They fill the Tonka with the cams from my mother's sewing machine, then dump them in a pile on the shag. My mother sighs as she reaches the stairs, considers turning out one of the lights.

65

The Sun

My mother, my mother, my mother, standing at the edge of the family room, her hands full of balled socks and books and empty glasses that need to go upstairs. After everyone is in bed, she decides, she will return to pick up the mess.

Memory shifts and slides. How much easier it is to send her to the lumberyard while Bryan dangles from the doorsill, to keep her in the kitchen while my father asks me to help him work on the car.

When I was maybe five years old, she sat with me until I fell asleep, holding my hands, running her fingers along my face, not allowing me to touch my vagina where pin worms scratched the sensitive folds of skin. Having called the doctor, she had dutifully placed Scotch tape across the entrance to ensnare the worms. Both bait and trap, I tried to keep my body still, please my mother with my ability not to scratch, all the while wanting to tear the tape away, free the worms, itch myself. The golden angel that she wound and placed beside my head remains on my dresser still, and every now and then I wind the key and listen to "Brahms' Lullaby," music that reminds me of worms and pain and my mother's piano-long fingers tracing the contour of my face.

I can recall the warmth of the bathroom, steam from the shower still clinging to the walls and the edges of the mirror, my mother with a half-slip pulled over her chest, leaning against the military-regulation porcelain sink, the eyelash curler holding captive both her eyelashes and my gaze. I sit on the closed lid to the toilet, knees pulled to chest, watching my mother get dressed for the evening—the navy's Birthday Ball, a Hail and Farewell, New Year's Eve. Blue Grass powder fills the room as she draws the sky-blue puff across arms, legs, and stomach, careful to avoid the places she has already applied lotion. Eye shadow the color of a bruise, blush that makes her cheekbones even more pronounced, waiting on lipstick until the moment she walks out the door on my father's arm, stopping for a second to apply red to her lips with a little brush that emerges from a thin gold container only to vanish again when she is done. We talk, our words mingling with steam and powder, lotion, and warmth from the blow dryer, about my friends, my day, the way I want to cut my hair. But mostly I just sit, skinny arms wrapped about my knees, watching as my mother moves with make-up and a mirror in a way I associate with gin and tonics, cigarettes, and dresses that drag the floor.

For most of my childhood my mother never wore jeans in public, could will away sickness, and feed a hundred people with as much apparent effort as she took to make the sack lunches my brothers and I carried every day to school. To say she was a saint is only to reiterate what my father said about her almost every day. And yet, I know such a mantle only reinforces the fairy tales my father liked to spin.

To fully see my mother, though, I would have to admit more than the fact that she made casseroles or believed yarn and felt would heal me. I would have to do more than detail the way she tilts her head for pictures, the same way I tilt mine, so that when the two of us are pictured together, our heads form a heart, hair falling between. It would not be enough to say her jewelry always matches her outfit in both tone and color or that she always puts her fork back on her plate between bites, so that she is always the last one done but the only one who eats with any awareness. I would also have to own the knowledge that she stood by as my father berated me as a child, that she allowed him to rage like a hurricane, and that she bore witness to an anger that wrapped my family in its arms and worked to suffocate us. I can't remember that mother. I find myself unable to take my mother, the angel, the sun itself, off the golden music box and ask her why she would let him rail that way.

What I have instead is the way she tickled my face when she tucked me into bed, her fingers grazing my cheeks and running along my forehead, letting me know she was there. Sometimes at night, after the lights were out and I was in bed, she would trace letters on my back in the dark, spelling the things in this world that I loved, the beach, my parents, the characters in books. One letter at a time, while I guessed, chaining them together, waiting for the last letter, not wanting the words to end. My mother's hands, touching and holding. And me begging her not to leave until I was asleep.

She would talk with me after my father had yelled. How many times did I lie on my narrow bed, room dark, face down and in tears, overrun by my father's words, his face, the way he held his arms, the blaming, the misunderstanding, the lack of boundaries, my own words, my anger, and my adolescent selfishness? A memory, so strong I can taste its bitterness, my tongue pushing against my teeth: my father on his knees, me on mine, the bed between us, you hate me, he yells, you hate me, and I am unable to respond.

Then my mother comes to me, sits beside me until my crying collapses to hiccups. She brushes the hair away from my face, feeds me the bread crumbs that will lead me back to my father for another evening, another morning, an entire day. "You can sometimes dislike those you love," she tells me, words that both confuse and comfort, words I hold like my pillow.

In the many months following Bryan's near drowning and before we moved to Seattle, my mother paid for a babysitter and drove across town so that she could move the limbs of a boy who hadn't been as lucky as my brother. This little boy hadn't slipped into the pool while his sister jumped through tires. He had simply been riding his trike. Maybe he was chasing a bug or the cat or a leaf that skittered across the driveway. Maybe he just stopped to look at the sky. Far from his mother's view, a garbage truck backed over him, crushing him beneath the weight of all that refuse. The boy was paralyzed from the neck down. No cast, no hole at his stomach where his mother could rub her fingers, he no longer moved.

My mother and others volunteered every week to move his body for him, in some vain hope that his tiny muscles would remember, would start moving on their own. Even then, I recognized her weekly trip as a kind of penance. She knew what could happen when you looked away.

At dinner, my mother rarely talked about what it was like to work with a boy who couldn't run like Bryan, couldn't talk like Bryan, couldn't even fix his eyes in one place. I imagine those mornings were spent in silence, small talk made even smaller in the face of such loss. Or perhaps it was the opposite. Maybe my mother tried even harder to carry the conversation, to make everyone comfortable as they gathered around a tiny body rather than a game board. Maybe the women shared recipes or exchanged ordinary worries. Maybe the mother of the paralyzed boy wanted things to seem as normal as possible, as if they were having coffee but without the cake.

On the rear window of the van, my mother glued a wide-angle mirror that helped her see what was behind her when she backed up. The pain of running over a child would be avoided, even if other pain could not be.

66

The Tree

For years, when they lived in Hawaii, her children fell like mangos, fell from mangos, and from plumeria, as well as from slides and poles and rope swings. Sometimes they broke when they hit the ground, sometimes not. She learned to keep their medical records in the drawer of the cabinet near the door rather than at the Navy Dispensary. Too often, the enlisted person was unable to locate the thick gray folder, while her child howled beside her.

Which was why, when her son Bryan, not yet five, walked up to her in Linda Thomas's yard holding a wrist that wilted like cooked spaghetti, she sent him home to inform his sister and find both his records and her purse. "I'll meet you at the car."

Linda's jaw dropped, she was sure, though she had turned her back by then and was headed home. What could Linda possibly understand? She and her husband had only recently had their first child, late into their thirties. The baby, Gregory, was asleep inside, and Linda had been asking if she thought he would forget his father.

"Each night," Linda said, picking at the gardening gloves she held in her hands, "I show Gregory a picture of Eric, tell him it's his daddy. Do you think that's enough?"

Linda's husband, the CO of a fast attack sub, had recently left for a six-month cruise. Gregory was only a few months old. When his father returned, he would be crawling.

"I think anything helps," she said, but she was lying. Of course her infant son wouldn't remember his father. How could this woman still inhabit a universe where things remained intact?

Her own children had all arrived damaged in one way or another, at least both Jennifer and Bryan, and if they hadn't arrived in the world broken, they soon found plenty of ways to fracture. She could remember bringing her daughter home, bound tightly in a sling that kept arm pasted to abdomen, how the lights in the incubator lit her son's blond hair so that he seemed to sleep in flame. She had known from the first moment of motherhood that will and determination were as essential as a sturdy stroller.

She looked up to see Bryan, holding his broken wrist with the good hand, call his sister's name. When he entered the narrow channel between the hibiscus hedge, she lost sight of him. It was two o'clock in the afternoon, just before the dry docks let out. Maybe the dispensary wouldn't be that busy yet.

"Linda," she said, turning back to the woman whose tightly kinked hair had recently started to gray, "I think Gregory will be fine."

Linda stood on the sidewalk, a pink hibiscus behind her, gloves loose in her palm.

When she got to the van, her daughter met her with the medical records and her macramé purse. Bryan sat in the back, his cheeks streaked with mud, his wrist supported by a long, thin board book they used to splint broken bones. He was crying.

"Don't worry, sweetheart," she said gently after taking the records and her purse from her daughter. "The doctors will make it all okay." Then she started the van and headed for the base.

67

The Garage

Toward the end of my freshman year in high school in
Virginia, we begin to build an attached two-car garage. Late
April, the Virginia sky looms gray and cold above us, the
light, dishwater-thin. As soon as my father thinks we have
passed the last snow, he drives to the lumber store with the
plans he and my mother have been drawing all winter and
buys more lumber than can fit atop the Caravan. Because it
involves laying a foundation, framing a structure, and roofing,
the garage is a major project. Every weekend and most nights
after school, we are expected to help. I have nowhere else to
be, still have no friends, so I help as well.

One afternoon, we are nailing plywood to the frame,
large sheets of wood that take all of us to hold in place. My
father works on the inside of the structure, while my mother
and I stand on the mounds of dirt we have cleared for the
foundation. We hold the sheets of wood against the two-by-
fours with our combined body weight. The dirt below our
feet is uneven, most of it piled from the trenches we dug
to make the foundation. Our shoes slip and slide amid the
crumbling pile of dirt.

"God damn it!" he yells, and by the sound of the hammer
we know he has missed his nail. "Scott, come and help me."

My brother stops loading the wheelbarrow with rocks and runs inside the frame.

"Hand me these nails."

As my mother and I stand together on the outside of the garage, my father and brother inside, we say nothing, look at the dirt, the sky, the oaks still empty of leaves. Only a few days before, my mother had taken me to Merle Norman and spent almost a hundred dollars on make-up for me, something she had been promising for years. I keep the eye shadows and blushes in their pink boxes, not wanting to mar the plastic finish. In the mornings I draw the three different eye shadows across my lids, first the lilac, then the darker purple, and then just a hint of green in the crease. I have contacts now as well, and I will often stand in front of the mirror, make-up on, and wonder how others see me. My mother has asked me not to tell my father how much it cost. "He wouldn't understand," she says, which meant, then, that she does understand, and, in understanding the cost of make-up, she also understands me. We stand holding the plywood sheets, sharing that kind of knowledge.

Inside the frame, my father curses and yells. Nothing will hold.

"Do you have it flat against the frame?" he asks.

We look at the plywood, push against it some more, and nod our heads.

"It is flat?" he yells again.

"Yes," we say in unison. I put my fingers to my eyelashes and try to separate a few lashes that have stuck together with the mascara. I feel the board slip.

Yesterday when we worked on the garage, my mother cried. When the tenth or fifteenth or twentieth load of red dirt she had wheelbarrowed from the piles around the garage

to the woods in back fell over and filled the recently cleared
trenches, she stood there under the gray sky and fell apart.
I watched her sob from the other side of the trenches, her
patched jeans covered in dirt, her sweatshirt loose and full
of holes. Even though my father rushed to right the wheelbarrow, to fill it again, we all knew the mess remained. After
a few minutes, she wiped her face and went into the house,
returning later with a cup of tea that sent strands of steam
into the air. Setting the mug on the roots of a nearby tree,
she grabbed the wheelbarrow and shovel and began to load
the dirt again. We said nothing.

"God damn it! Who is not holding the board?" my father
yells.

With both hands and my whole body, I press against the
board, feel the plank bow under our weight. My mother
looks at me, our cheeks set against the rough board, and
we hold each other's gaze. Under the gray sky, her blue eyes
are startling but warm. The edges of her mouth turn up, the
beginning of a grin.

Inside my father carries on, first yelling at Scott, then the
board, then the lines we drew in pencil.

Outside, though, my mother and I start to laugh. Flakes of
snow have started falling, making the dirt even more slippery
under our feet. We start sliding down the hill, our feet unable
to find purchase on the slope, while we struggle against
gravity to hold the board. Our shoes skitter, our hold lessens,
the board drifts an inch, then we right it. The plywood walls
block my father and his anger, and our laughter buries his
sound. There is a kind of comic insanity in holding up a wall
with only our weight, a madness in the slipperiness of the
mud. Under a gray sky that spits flecks of snow at our cheeks,
for a moment we find a space beyond his anger, our bodies

shaking against the walls, the wind scraping our cheeks, our chins. In that place, laughter is the only response to rage.

68

The Deep

Count the waves, close your eyes, ignore the fingernail polish, hammer your pet pig's skull, move, then move again, and again, and again, hold these boards straight, no these boards, no these boards, and then hold the kitten underwater until it no longer struggles in your hand, choose your wife, your daughter, the navy, choose your husband, hide the fact that you see double, play the ace; the nurse is burning your baby, your son, your brother is hanging by a thread, or is that you, your father is raping your sister, and the admiral wants you in Hawaii, a signature orders you to move; take this parking place, no this one, and then resign yourself to farming for the rest of your life, run your body into the ground, don't eat that apple, that cheese, that chocolate shake, hit the fish hard, on its head, shatter its eyeball, here is the red button, push it, here is the boy who laughed at you, stab, here is the father who yelled at you because his father yelled at him and the mother who watched, a dish towel thrown over her shoulder like a scarf, you are in a bucket, in the bushes, under a wave.

Grant me a divorce, drown the kittens, anticipate the tool. I will give you a reason to be afraid. In the simmering sea, there is no pocket, no space where the good guys win because even the good guys are bad guys, after all, you can dislike those you love, and sometimes, just sometimes you can laugh. You cannot sort the pennies any longer, the stacks topple on a table made by your father, the boards won't fit. No matter how hard you try the boards won't fit. He cannot save you, and not because you can't be saved but because the sun is in his eyes or he is at work and you are underwater, belly up, chlorine filling your lungs. The surface is above you; see the way the sun cuts through the water and sends its beams to the ocean floor. Swim for the surface, keep your eyes closed, ignore the churning of the ocean, the pressure in your ears, and swim. And if you can't swim, then laugh, because the snow is coming down harder and the dirt has turned to flame, the wheelbarrow can't be righted, and the dry docks haven't let out.

69

The Road

To college, I bring what fits in two suitcases. While other students carry boxes filled with posters, stereos, and worn stuffed animals up the dorm stairs, my mom and I drive to the grocery and buy sodas for the mini-fridge. We have flown from Honolulu, where our family has been relocated once again, through LA, and then to Denver. We rent a car and drive. The University of Nebraska in Lincoln sits about four thousand miles from my family, half a continent and the Pacific Ocean in between. After two days, my mother will return to Hawaii to be with my brothers when they start the school year, and I will sit on my twin bed and stare at the mustard-colored walls of my dorm room. What had accompanied me in previous moves becomes reduced to the voices, worn thin from the journey under the ocean floor, of my parents when I call home on Sundays. At breakfast, I eat furtively in the dorm cafeteria, hoping no one sees me eating alone. Lunch and dinner I skip. Below the earth's surface, in the cinderblock basement of my dormitory, I jump rope for hours. The black metal spring that binds the middle of the spongy rope hisses like a cat each time it comes in contact with the concrete floor.

Because I am without other military dependents, commissaries, or ports in which to moor, I run. I run from the "freshman fifteen" and fraternity parties where boys roll quarters down their noses and laugh as they chug clear plastic cups full of warm beer. I run from the hard gray winters of the plains that leave me depressed and pining for the sun. I run from a Greek system that organizes mandatory social functions where I have to listen to fraternity pledges sing puerile songs. I run from a lack of boundaries, borders, and edges and from the fear of sitting still. I run for the same reasons I no longer eat: my body is what I can control.

Far from campus, I run to neighborhoods where no one knows me, one-story brick houses and broken sidewalks lining my path. Running past the capitol and around the state fairgrounds, I measure success in terms of mileage and calories burned. At the end of each run, I sprint up the ten flights of stairs to my dorm floor. In the empty stairwell, my footfalls echo, and I pound my way to the top. Reaching my room, I record on a slip of paper another five miles alongside the lettuce I have eaten for lunch. These pieces of paper I keep hidden in my drawer, taking them out at night and counting and recounting the totals, reading them repeatedly as if they are letters from home.

I don't remember the first day I decided to go running. Throughout high school, I played sports after school but never track. I certainly didn't own running shoes when I arrived in Lincoln. My new roommate, Lisa, though, runs, and maybe that's where I get the idea. I also know she purges, and while I can't bring myself to stick a finger down my throat, I can deny my body food. It is easy. After years of eating by myself in school cafeterias, I am more than happy to avoid the shame of a long, empty table and a book propped in front of my tray. I don't have a car or money. If I miss meal times, I miss my only chance at food.

At night, I move my hands along my shrinking belly, feel the bones of my rib cage, the taut skin. I love the elemental feel of my body, bones and skin, as lean as a submarine. By the end of my first semester, I weigh less than a hundred pounds. My period stops but I do not. When I cannot run because of a blizzard or a bruised ankle, I jump rope entire afternoons. Every day I weigh myself, my body dissolving like salt in water.

"You are so tiny," a stranger says to me at a party, beer in hand. "When you turn sideways you disappear."

70

The Cowgirl

We stand in the dorm bathroom, one day, every day, each in our own stall. She in the one next to me. I can see her sandals, her toes painted red. I wear tennis shoes with grass stains. It is spring, warming, and girls sunbathe on the lawn between the dorms. No light enters the bathroom, brown tiled walls and the smell of mildew and cleanser.

I can't tell if she is crying or if those muffled sounds suggest something other than tears. I am crying, though, without a sound. And I haven't even brought my finger to my mouth. Is this how you do it, I wonder, one finger, or several, and how far down? I don't ask her, the girl in the stall down from me, because we are pretending to be in the bathroom peeing. At the right moment, we will flush the toilet to conceal the sounds of our bodies giving up the food we only recently consumed.

But I can't do it. I try, but I can't. How many times have I stood in this stall garnering the strength to take action? How many times have I traced the grout between the tiles with my eyes, turning corner after corner down the wall? My body wretches as soon as I put a finger down my throat and the clenching of stomach and throat is so final, so fierce, that I am scared to push any farther, imagine consuming myself from the outside in. The toilet down the way flushes; I see her sandals turn and leave. Soon I am alone in the bathroom, sitting on the toilet, hating my body, wanting to rip into my skin, beat my legs, my stomach, my fingers that won't go down. For what seems like hours, I sit on the toilet and wait for the strength to let it all go. Steam from the showers turns the air moist and wet, and I am returned to Mrs. Hansen's bathroom. Almost ten years later, and I don't need her to take me by the hand. I require no help in finding the stains.

71

The Doctor

The summer after my first year in college, I return to Hawaii where my family is still stationed. My father is the lawyer for the entire Pacific Fleet now. In a year, he will be eligible to make admiral. To get to my house, I pass through guard gates, concrete barricades, and over speed bumps filled with explosives.

One morning I tell my mother that my period has stopped. She seems concerned, but not overly, and she makes an appointment for me to see a doctor later in the summer. When the day of the appointment arrives, I feel a kind of relief. I know the doctor will take one look at my skeletal body and name my eating disorder aloud. He will tell my parents, and I will have to get help. A year of relentless denial has exhausted me. My daily outlook depends on how little I eat. The days when I hardly have the energy to run are the days I feel my best. Deep down, I wonder how long I can keep this all up.

The doctor is male, in his mid-forties, with brown curly hair. He wears glasses and a watch that fits loosely at his wrist. Because the face of the watch always hangs down, it is clear he has little need to know the time.

I sit on the white paper of the examination table, a thin gown tied in three bows at my back. He has listened to my heart, rapped on my belly, looked in my ears.

"Lots of young women have irregular periods," he says, quoting almost word for word what my mother has told me.

I nod my head.

He takes up his clipboard and scratches some notes.

"It's really nothing to worry about. I'm going to give you a prescription for birth control pills. They can help regulate your period."

"But," I say, "my period isn't irregular. It's stopped."

"Yes, I know," he says and continues to look down at the clipboard. "That means it's irregular."

I can feel the draft from the air conditioner as it meets my bare back. Goosebumps rise on my skin; the tiny hairs covering my arms are much longer than they used to be in my body's effort to keep me warm. I shiver.

"Could it be related to eating?" I offer.

"Could what?" He stops now, his watch swaying like a pendulum, the pen returned to the pocket of his white coat.

"My period. Could it be related maybe to how much I eat?" It is the closest I can get, close enough, I think, for a doctor to see through. I can't understand how this man can sit in front of me, my naked body as thin as the robe that covers it, and not put two and two together.

"Not at all. It's really common in young women, nothing to worry about." And he rips off the top sheet of his prescription pad, handing the white paper to me. "Just take these pills."

I carry the prescription in my purse back to college and never fill it.

The pill often causes weight gain.

72

The Phone Call

Spring break of my sophomore year in college, I go home with my friend Paige to her farm in far western Nebraska. When I run the dirt roads near her house, I run to Colorado and back. I have never been on a farm, never been eight miles from a carton of milk, never gotten lost while running because the corn grows so tall around me that I have no bearings at all. Paige and I have a great time, seeing Cheyenne, walking the dirt roads, visiting her relatives. I spend most of the week with my mouth open in astonishment at what the plains feel like.

Only at the end of the week do I learn that Paige has other reasons for inviting me home. A recovering bulimic, she knows the signs of an eating disorder and insists that I call my parents and get help. From her living room window, I can see the green fields with their tasseled burdens. Paige sits beside me as the phone rings on Oahu, thousands of miles away, hours earlier, where my family is just getting up for the day.

As usual, both my parents get on the phone when they find out it is me. They drop whatever they are doing and ask me how I am. Their brightness is fine-edged and sharp. I imagine my way to Hawaii, trying to peer through the phone cord and into their lives, routines I used to know, routines that

I used to participate in but that in the past two years have shifted and changed to accommodate one less person. I no longer know the rhythms of their days. I am not even sure which rooms they are in when they talk to me. Our conversations seem to float in space, groundless, untethered.

"Mom, Dad," I say nervously, as Paige nudges my leg. I have spent the first ten minutes telling them about the farm, putting off the hard stuff. My dad is eager to hear all the details; he compares the Mellors' farming operation with the one of his childhood. I know I need to cut in before he starts recalling stories from his boyhood days. "I wanted to talk about something."

They wait on the other end of the line. Paige moves closer to me on the couch that we are sharing. In the kitchen, the door opens and her mother returns from picking up Paige's sister. The car keys rattle as they hit the counter, then the thud of something solid, like groceries, on the wooden table. Turning my back away from the noise, I look at Paige again, hoping she will indicate I can end the conversation because her family has come home. She looks determined, her green eyes narrow but gentle.

In high school, when she was bulimic, she ate laxatives rather than food. No more than five feet, Paige had been tiny her whole life but never tiny enough. By the time I met her in college, she had recovered. At school, I watched her eat with envy. She never ate a lot, but meals didn't cause her anxiety. Three times a day, she walked through the line at the cafeteria and filled her plate. When she told me it was time to tell my parents about my own relationship to food, I trusted her. And as I had felt with the doctor, I thought maybe, if I said something, I would get help. In Paige's full cafeteria tray, I saw a possible future.

Paige's mother and sister head back outside, their voices dimming as they shut the front door. The house grows quiet again; outside, a sea of corn tosses against the blue, blue sky. The expanse of green and the dance of stalks reminds me of the ocean, how it never settles, never stills. I feel closer to my parents, both surrounded by seas.

"I'm not eating," I say, and I can feel my body relax, the couch cushions almost sinking with me. Before they can say anything, I plow on. I explain how little I eat, how much I exercise. I tell them about my weight, my period, the way food, or its lack, runs my life. For several minutes, I talk without stopping, my heart pounding, tears in my eyes, and Paige right beside me, her hand on my leg.

When I finish, I am not sure what I expect. Anger I think. Maybe concern or shock. I wait, the emptiness of the line making the distance between us magnify.

"Well," my mother says finally, "you just need to eat."

73

The Pig

For the first few years after my parents were married, they lived in Lincoln, Nebraska, while my father finished law school. Quite possibly, they lived in one of the brick houses I pass every day on my run.

To pay for school, my father hired on as a fireman for the railroad. He spent his summer riding the same rails his father took to leave home when he was twelve, a line of track that ferried Sinor men from boyhood to manhood. He could make as much money riding the rails for three months as my mother could garner in a solid year of secretarial work at Nebraska Educational Television.

A hundred years ago, the work of a fireman was backbreaking and dangerous. On a steam engine, he shoveled coal into the boiler of the engine to create steam, making sure the fire remained strong and hot. The job required that he knew the route, could gauge the amount of steam needed, and could generate that fuel by raising or banking the fire. My father worked on diesel engines and didn't shovel coal, though that didn't make the job any safer, nor did it mean he didn't work with fire. Part of his job was to monitor the left side of the train, watching the wheels on the hot boxes to make sure they didn't catch fire and derail the train. Custom saw the fireman as an apprenticeship to engineer and often he took over when the engineer, or hog head, wanted to rest. In those moments, my father was in charge of the entire train.

To make the money he needed to make, my father was always on call. He could be asked to report to work within twenty-four hours and then remained awake for days at a time. He rode a dangerous section of rail from Kearney to Burwell. While most routes in the country run east-west, the Kearney-Burwell route runs north-south. This meant the train constantly passed through intersections where crossing arms had not been installed and people weren't expecting a train. The engineer he rode with most often, Whistling Willie, had killed some twenty-nine people on that route alone. Whistling Willie rode from Kearney to Burwell constantly blowing the whistle in hopes of avoiding the thirtieth.

Many evenings my father found himself in a small town in Nebraska for a few hours, waiting for the return route. On these nights, Willie often persuaded him to down half pints of Canadian Club in one swallow along with the other men in the crew. A month earlier he had been in a classroom arguing an esoteric point of federal court jurisdiction, now he tried to hold his own with men who had seen automobiles fly to pieces on impact.

One night, deep into a summer of work, his body strong and muscled from helping to load freight, he was called to serve clean-up for a train that had derailed in the middle of nowhere. Under a moonless sky, twisted metal and train cars lay bent and crippled in a wheat field at the end of August, waiting to burn. My father spent the entire night working by headlamp, the beam catching glimpses of train detritus— handles, panels, the lunchbox carried by one of the railwaymen. Sometimes he could get beneath the wreckage; sometimes he could free a door, enter a window. More often, though, he left entire cars unsearched, knowing it would have to wait for daylight and heavy machinery. Every now and then he heard a coyote call across the plains and waited for his mate to answer. When she did, he thought of his wife, home in bed asleep, untouched by wreckage and death. This was what she feared when she drove him to the depot each night for work, that his train would fail to follow its course, would refuse to remain on the rails.

What people didn't realize when they saw a mighty locomotive was just how fragile the engine was, a front end made mostly of tin. On impact, the engine collapsed as did the bodies inside. More than once he had already had to "go to the floor" when a collision looked imminent. He dreaded telling her about this one.

For hours he worked, sweat gathering under his armpits and running in a line along his spine. Often he worked alone. A breeze blew across the fields every now and then bringing a chill to his bare arms and forehead. Deep into the night, weary from the hauling and pulling and the walking and lifting, he spotted a leather glove that had fallen near the engine, a man's glove, the kind firemen wore to protect their hands from the hot metal and rough edges. When he bent down to retrieve it, he found the glove filled with a hand. In his own hand, the fingered glove seemed to return his grasp.

What did he do? Drop it? Set it on the ground? Hold it even more tightly? Did he call out to a fellow searcher or just carry the hand the length of the train? Maybe he determined to look harder for the body of its owner, thinking a man should be buried whole. Or maybe he placed the hand on the overturned engine and walked away, unable to own the reality, wanting only the knowledge bound in law books. Or maybe he buried the hand in a shallow grave, not unlike the syringes from long ago. Most likely, he placed the severed hand in the drawer beside the kittens and the pig, locked it, then got in the car and drove home.

74

The Uniform

"Just eat," her mother says because the mind controls the body.

"Just eat," her mother says because we must do our duty to the corps.

"Just eat," her mother says because the trains must run on time.

Or at least that is what the daughter hears. She doesn't hear her mother pleading with her only daughter who is an ocean away to take care of herself. She doesn't hear her father trying to embrace her through the phone.

THE SUMMER AFTER I graduated from high school in Hawaii, a serial killer began murdering young women on the Pali Highway, a road that cut across the mountains and joined Honolulu to the windward side of the island. From the local swap meet, the killer had purchased a flashing blue light which he displayed on the dashboard of his car just like Steve McGarrett did on *Hawaii Five-0*. He stopped women on the highway wearing the stolen uniform of a police officer. First, he pulled them over with his flashing light, then he got them to leave their cars. These two props—the whirling light and the uniform—were enough to lure victim after victim into the dark and viney kudzu along the road.

I drove the Pali regularly because my boyfriend lived in Kailua. His curfew was earlier than mine, so I often drove home at night. As young woman after young woman slipped from this world in a bloody and violent way, my father became more aggressive in his advice. At first I was to keep the windows rolled up if the police ever stopped me. Soon, though, he was telling me never to stop for anyone, including the police, to just drive to the nearest police station and take the matter up there. "If all else fails," he said, one night at the dinner table after learning a fourth woman had died, "if for some reason you find yourself out of the car and in danger, then run."

He looked at me when he said this, his napkin taken from his lap and set next to his plate. The candles on the table flickered in the dark room and threw shadows of my family on the white walls.

"Run?" I asked, trying to imagine myself on the Pali Highway, a dark strip of road without streetlights or buildings, a jungled blackness.

"Your legs," he says, "are your best weapon."

75

The Winnie

I return home to Hawaii the summer before my junior year.
Once my brothers are done with school, in late June, my
family flies back to the mainland for a trip my parents have
orchestrated: two months driving across the country, all in
a Winnebago the size of a barn. I am twenty. My brother
Scott, seventeen, Bryan, fourteen. That September the Berlin
Wall will fall, ending the Cold War and my military childhood. At twenty-one, I will no longer be a military depen-
dent, and I will be engaged.

My father's original plan for our trip, his lifelong dream
in fact, had been to sail around the world with his family in
a small boat of some sort, but either because of the cost of
watercraft or the fact that four of the five of us don't know
how to sail, he and my mom choose instead to cruise the
interstates of America armed with a *Let's Go* guide as thick
as my fist.

The five of us begin in the middle of the country. After
flying from Hawaii to Kansas City, we take a small plane to
Grand Island, Nebraska, where we visit my aunt and uncle
and pick up the Winnebago. Our route carves a giant figure
eight beginning with a month exploring the East Coast and
then finishing the trip in the West. Beyond that, we have
little sense of a plan. Over the dinner table, weeks before

we leave, my parents compare our upcoming adventure to their years in Asia. No maps, no guidebooks, and no reservations, they would simply wake up in the morning and decide to take a train across India or wander toward Vietnam or hole up in Singapore for a week. We set off that summer with heady ideas.

It is my second trip in the Winnie. Twelve years earlier, in the summer of 1978, before my family moved back to Hawaii from Seattle, we traveled around the Pacific Northwest with my grandparents in their new-to-them Winnebago. As a child, the Winnie was a place of wonders, full of secret drawers and cubbies and an elaborate system of latches that kept everyone and everything from falling while on the road. Tables converted into beds, mattresses slid from the walls, and you could sleep in a loft perched above the driver's head and watch the world pass by through a narrow window that opened with a crank. The tiny refrigerator, the square sink, and the stove that slept beneath a removable countertop were constant delights to me, and I loved running the short length of hallway in one direction and knowing we were driving in another.

At twenty, though, I no longer see the charm. The table is now where I sleep, and every night I have to clear away a day's worth of crumbs and papers to begin making my bed. We take showers while the Winnie is moving, so that the gray water can drain onto the interstate without anyone knowing. I sit on the toilet, turn on the water that smells like baking soda, wet myself down, turn off the water, lather up, and then rinse off, all the time trying not to slip and fall while the Winnie barrels eastward. Often, due to negligence on the driver's part or the one showering, water soaks the roll of toilet paper, leaving us to peel wet tissue for days.

We brush our teeth while moving, pee while moving, sleep while moving, and eat while moving. My father believes in making time. To that end, we drive all night most nights. Sometimes, toward the morning when all of us, except Bryan, have taken a turn at the wheel and none of us can remain awake any longer, my dad pulls into a Chamber of Commerce parking lot, or a rest stop, or the side of the road and the Winnie stops. For those short hours, the only movement is the breathing of my family, five bodies within spitting distance of one another, trying to drift away.

THE URGENCY WITH which my dad drives across the country in the Winnie makes it seem as if we are hunted. Twenty hours of driving, thirty, fifty even, is not uncommon. We arrive at each new destination exhausted, especially my father, and often, having delivered us to the renovated mining town or the gardens or the geysers, he remains in the Winnie to sleep while the rest of us tour. Making time matters.

In addition, we break down almost daily. We spend the first day of our trip at PJ's Wrecker in Williamsburg, Iowa, trying to find new tires for the Winnie. While PJ works on the back end of the camper, my mom and I run the dirt roads that skirt the farms. Herds of cows accompany us as we make our way up and down the gentle hills; they only stop at the fence line or when it becomes clear we have no food to offer them. I am happy to trade the already cramped quarters of the camper for the vaulted expanse of the midwestern sky. Within several hours, we are on the road again, two new tires and the possibility of a shower now that we are moving.

Over the course of two months, we will replace each of the six tires but only after a blowout sends the Winnie off the side of the road accompanied by a tearing noise that sounds like a crashing jet. Once I am the one driving when we lose a tire, and my reaction is not to slow down but rather to duck. The tires are spring loaded and require special equipment to remove them, hence the all-day odysseys to find a mechanic who can help us out. What this also means is that whenever my father and brother are working on the wheels, they risk a tire exploding with the force of a cannon. The Winnie holds my family hostage on the plains.

By the time we hit New York, it is fairly clear that my father is not going to relax, as my mother promised me before we left. Nothing works right. We get lost, the refrigerator opens and spills its contents, the chosen sewer dump is already full and spews the contents of our toilet across the concrete, my dad hits his head on the bunk, we miss the ferry, the turn, the sign, the site. It is as though we are cursed.

Each day brings new burdens. Once, in Boston, we are packed in traffic and lost. The Freedom Trail has proven a tourist trap, our guide dubbed an idiot by my father, and the Liberty Bell, we discover, rests more than a day's drive away. Having sat for hours in the July heat, the Winnie offers little comfort. Several times we miss the turn we need for the tunnel and have to go back, each reversal accompanied by a more elaborate string of expletives. The narrow Boston roads make my dad nervous. How to navigate a barn-sized camper through streets built for carts and horses? While the colonists betray a level of short-sightedness only apparent to my father, my mom and I strain our eyes looking for the sign to the tunnel.

Finally, we find the highway and its twentieth-century widths, though the traffic makes the pavement seem less abundant. In order to get enough sleep to drive through the night, my father reluctantly turns the wheel over to Scott and heads for the back. For a few minutes, we resume our Winnie-on-the-road occupations. My mom and I sit at the kitchen table and play gin while Scott and Bryan listen to Love and Rockets and watch the pale Bostonian drivers work to pass the giant camper. The dark green curtains gently sway with the movement of the Winnie, pulling on their plastic tethers like dogs.

The silence doesn't last long. Scott isn't driving the way my dad wants, not fast enough or slow enough or gentle enough, and soon my father comes striding up from the back, rubbing his eyes against the afternoon light, yelling for Scott to get out of the driver's seat. Four long steps and he makes it to the front. He stands in the area just behind the front seats, his face red with anger.

"Get out," he says to Scott, "now." He grabs the green captain's chair and starts to swivel it in his direction. Scott looks to my mom, wondering, I suppose, if he should really leave the driver's seat open.

My mom begins, "But Morris—"

As Scott starts to move from the seat, I jump in "Dad, we are—"

No one finishes their sentences, though, because my father is pulling Scott from the seat.

In the middle of the highway, cars all around us, Scott leaves the steering wheel like he might his jacket, the driver's seat empty, the Winnie beaming down the road. When my dad goes to grab the steering wheel, he trips on a shoe and falls. From the floor of the camper he catches the edge of the wheel that is available to him and pulls. The Winnie now banks sharply to the right, cabinets popping open, plates and napkins raining down on our card game. Having regained his feet, my father overcompensates by pulling to the left and we go flying in the opposite direction. The Winnie rocks violently back and forth, barely able to stay upright. In my memory, Boston drivers are skidding everywhere to avoid being smashed by the giant Winnebago. Cars spin in circles, grind to a halt, and hurtle onto the shoulder in our wake. Inside the Winnie, once we recover a balanced position on the road, my dad yells about the shoe and the missed tunnel and the narrow Bostonian roads. The rest of us sit numbly at the table, surrounded by dinnerware, the *Let's Go* book in the door well as if trying to get out.

76

The Train

In New York City, we manage to secure cheap tickets to *The Phantom of the Opera*, but we each have to sit alone. The production lets out at 10:30 p.m., the city sky dark but, for the first time that day, clear of rain. Perhaps it is the clarity of the air that makes my dad decide we can make the 10:40 train at Grand Central Station. Having arrived at a split-second decision and pleased by the prospect of making such a tight connection, he sends Scott ahead to "hold the train," yelling at the back of my already running brother, "track 17." The rest of us take off in the same direction, jostling our souvenirs, playbills, and cheap umbrellas. Within several blocks, we make the station but almost immediately find that our train leaves from track 21; in fact, our train is getting ready to pull away. Meanwhile, Scott is waiting for us to meet him on 17. Pushing a wad of cash into my hand, my dad tells my mom, Bryan, and me to use our bodies as blockades to keep the doors from closing while he goes and retrieves Scott.

The certainty with which my father suggests we can stop the train makes wedging my body between the doors seem logical. With my foot against the tired rubber bumper pads and my back against the other door already impatient to shut, I try to ignore the electronic voice telling me to "step away from the doors." The doors become more insistent, and

I watch in terror as the doors close against my body, people yelling, the voice on the loudspeaker, no longer electronic, ordering us to "Clear the doors! Clear the doors! Clear the doors!" and in the distance my dad running for track 17, the poster from Les Mis slapping his thigh.

Looking back twenty years later, I cannot help but wonder why we didn't stop at a coffee shop to talk about the play and wait an hour for the next train. But we were making time. Those visions of wandering from one city to the next poking about in sleepy towns and bumping into wonderful restaurants faded further on the horizon. The one time my mother was a little crazy and took a detour into a town that held what in family lore has become "the world's largest ball of twine," my dad threw the atlas in anger. While we had thought there wasn't a plan, a set way of doing things, a specific way to trek across the country, there was. And my dad held both map and key.

77

The Mirror

Things are supposed to get better when we leave the East Coast and head west. My mom feels that the pace and expense of the East Coast chafe at my father and make him unhappy. Once we regain the open spaces of the prairies, land long familiar to him, he will worry less about the cost of museums and amusement parks and focus instead on the beauty before us. By the time we hit Nebraska, my dad has become sick. The stress and worry of the past month, or the torrential rains we have come upon once we cross the Mississippi, have finally settled in his lungs and nasal passages. A late start out of Cozad means we don't fill the spare tire with air. Right outside of Ogallala we blow another tire. Two hours of work on the side of the road and the help of some strangers allow us to hobble to the next town. Two hours later we have a new tire and are back on the road. By the time we reach my Uncle Jerry's house in Denver it is close to midnight. The next morning, we are supposed to head out bright and early for our first backpacking trip.

Either lack of sleep or altitude causes most everyone in my family to feel ill the following morning. The drive to the trailhead is punctuated with bouts of Bryan throwing up. Every few miles, we pull the car over and Bryan leans out the window. At one point on the trail we temporarily lose my brother when he passes out in a field of wildflowers, unable to walk another step. By the end of the first day, everyone in my family is throwing up except me. Their bodies are used to breathing at sea level and the air is too thin in the mountains. To make matters worse, we have gotten lost and can't find the right lake. Because my family has only car camped in the past and never backpacked, we have packed poorly, filling our backpacks with heavy jeans and too many changes of clothes. On the final push up a hill to our campsite, hip belts digging into our bones, we are reduced to counting thirty steps and resting, then thirty more. By flashlight, we set up camp. That night it begins to rain and does not stop for four days.

AFTER SEVERAL WEEKS hiking in Canada and a few days touring some of the national parks, we return to where we started, the heart of the nation, the Winnie spinning along on its new set of tires. During those final days my mother contracts conjunctivitis, we spend a day fighting the summer traffic in Yellowstone, and my dad spends $200 on a rafting trip that we all decide was not much fun. At our campsite near the Kicking Horse River the evening after our expensive rafting trip, the Winnie trip comes to a grinding halt.

Dinner ends and Bryan is gathering wood for a campfire. The metal door to the Winnie slaps shut each time my mother carries another load of dishes into the tiny kitchen. Inside, Scott and I read books by the thin light offered by the generator, moving every now and then to unstick our legs and arms from the vinyl bench seats.

On my way out the door, leaving the little light that we have, I step on a mirror and break it—a framed rectangular mirror, a tool really, that my dad has been using all summer to fix the Winnie, sliding it into the depths of the engine in hopes of seeing behind and between. It is August third, less than two weeks before the end of our trip. Scott had been told by my father earlier in the evening to pick up the tools.

When my father finds out, he explodes, somehow growing even larger in body as he falls apart.

"Who left this here?" he yells, though we all know.

"Who did this?"

Feet astride the broken glass, he rages at the sky, at us, at a universe that deals repeated injustices.

The Winnebago rocks, my seat seeming to vibrate. Stooping in the shadowless night, he picks up the glass and throws pieces in every direction. They strike the windows, the table, the cabinets above the sink. I duck my head, even though he is not aiming for me. Angered by expense, the lack of decent signage, construction, full sewer dumps, and children who whine about getting out of the camper to see more trees, frustrated with tools, and tires, and Winnies that fail to work properly, sick of children who never listen, complain of long drives, and seem to only want a hot shower and McDonald's, and tired with all the pushing, pulling, earning, driving, scaling, humping, pleading, whining, falling, failing, he snaps.

My brothers and I scatter in all directions. Whatever it is that for six weeks has been allowing us to keep coming back, to return to the breakfast table in the morning after hearing how much time we have lost, to laugh an hour after my father rages about the cost of ice cream cones in New York, to reassemble as a family even when all the forces in the world seem to be breaking us apart, whatever it is that allows me to once write in my journal following another incident, "I ended up in tears but it was good," is broken. I run to a rock in the middle of a stream where I sit and furtively watch the moon rise behind a dark green curtain of trees. Along the instep of my foot, I still feel the mirror cracking.

At some point my dad finds me. His face matches the sound of the crickets, worn and grated smooth, force of will replaced by surrender. He says, "I want to go home."

78

The Teacher

At sixteen he had learned everything he could from the teacher in the one-room schoolhouse. He had been listening to the lessons meant for older children, seizing knowledge like a life preserver, desperate to keep afloat. His oldest brother, Jerry, the one he would always revere, had left for college the previous year. Bill, his next older brother, ran the farm. Two paths opened before him, two ways of living in the world.

The day of high school graduation, his teacher took him aside, moments before the actual ceremony, bringing him to the side of the building where the afternoon sun had just begun to sink down the brick.

"Red," he asked, "what are your plans?"

"Dunno," he answered, "go to college maybe," a response that surprised him as he spoke it, coming from some deep and inarticulate space inside but arriving as familiar as the schoolhouse itself.

"College?" his teacher asked. "You're not Jerry."

"I know," he said, ready to explain the still-forming idea of studying business, maybe to return to the farm, maybe not.

"You're a farmer, Red, like your father. You will never be more than that. Ever."

The teacher, a man perhaps who saw student after student return to the farm, who maybe had long ago given up hope that any might leave, or maybe just a man whose own failures caused him to want the same for those around him, turned, eager to rejoin the ceremony, leaving my father with a future of corn and soil, the same corn and soil that bankrupted his father and left the family teetering on the edge of penury.

He will spend his entire life finishing the conversation. He had been raised to be a farmer. His father never finished fourth grade. His mother had only a few more years of education. What they had was land, soil. So even though the land his family owned could not possibly support the four sons once they were men, he had given little thought to being anything else. At that moment, faced with a man insisting he had limits, he vowed never to work a field again.

AT VARIOUS POINTS in my life, usually when I was asking if I could work fewer hours at the mall or resign as an officer of some organization or another, my father had reminded me of the importance of "being the best that ever was" in whatever I undertook. "Make sure," he would tell me, "once you leave a job, people long afterwards say that Jennifer Sinor was the best that ever was." It didn't matter if I was taking orders at Wally Wok or running the country. As an example, he would offer his own career, jobs he had held where no one had ever matched his skill or service, compliments he had received, awards he had won.

That is so arrogant, I would think. But arrogance had nothing to do with it, though poverty might have.

Life, my father thought, hinged on certain pivotal moments, moments that defined or destroyed you, and who you were depended on how you responded.

THE SUMMER MY family drove across the country in a Winnebago the size of a barn, my father tried to outrun his pain. But we could not drive fast enough. In almost every state, we ended up lost, the tiny map in the *Let's Go* book failing to lead us to the right destination again and again.

I did not wonder then why my father took two months of vacation when he had never taken two weeks. I did not wonder where he was that summer as he sat in the captain's seat piloting the Winnie like a spacecraft. Only much later would I realize that our trip coincided with the fact that he had not been promoted to admiral. He had not been selected for "flag" and his twenty-plus-year career in the military was over. For the first time in his professional life, he had not been the best that ever was. I did not know this was what hunted us that summer. Perhaps if I had turned around and looked behind us, I might have seen failure keeping pace, never lagging, a shape I would have known as intimately as my own belly.

79

The Boy

The fall after the Winnie trip, I looked forward to returning to the order I had created at school, my father safely fenced by the telephone call each weekend, no longer carping about the price of fuel. Even my eating disorder, though still central to my life, had become a kind of gentle hum that accompanied me to and from class. I had perfected the control of my body to a scientific level, just like counting waves in the ocean. As long as I didn't deviate from the program, I could weigh myself on the scale inside my mind.

One early fall day, light bouncing off the linoleum tiles of the Nebraska Union, students rushing past carrying backpacks full of books with unbroken spines, I shook Steven's hand for the first time. He wore tie-dyed pants that billowed at his thighs and a shirt rumpled in a studied way. I had just been named a leader for the student programming board, and Steven was my mentor. He was twenty-five and living with a woman named Ann. His eyes were the exact color of the sea.

I could never have imagined that Steven liked me. He was too handsome, too assured, wore sunglasses inside. He had hung out backstage with the Rolling Stones, while I still listened to Hall and Oates. We lived in different worlds.

But almost every day, I ran across campus from my Romantics class, my heart full of Keats and Shelley and the way Steven's mouth turned up at the corners when he smiled, and I sat with him in his cubicle, surrounded by signed pictures of Paula Abdul and Eddie Van Halen. Just being in his space made me feel important, worthwhile.

One night he and his friend Mike came to my sorority house. I was away at one of many meetings. My friend Kerry left a note for me on the message board: "Steven and Mike stopped by to see you. They sure were cute, Jen, esp. Steven." And that's when I realized he might like me.

By January he was sending me cards: "You are turning me into a morning person because I can't wait to get up and see you." I saved everything, every piece of evidence that said I was chosen: three cards on Valentine's because he couldn't decide between them, notes that praised my hair, flowers left in my car, the receipt for every dinner, every movie, every motel, champagne corks, matchbooks, "Do Not Disturb" signs from motels in Denver, Kansas City, small towns in Wisconsin. At night I would sort through them, organizing them by date, by event, by the way they made me feel. Each was a response to my fears of never being enough that I could hold in my hand.

Almost a year after I met Steven, we had sex. In part, I worried I would lose him if I didn't. I justified my decision by assuming we would get married, so that through some crazy calculus my loss of virginity didn't count. But in addition, a growing part of me had become tired of the rules and self-imposed limits of my world and wanted to give in to my body. The actual experience felt undramatic, some pain and little pleasure. We were visiting Mike in Minnesota. I like to remember us lying on a makeshift bed set in a bay window overlooking the city of St. Paul, red blankets surrounding us, green leaves popping at eye level. More likely, though, we were in a windowless second bedroom, crowded between bicycles or rowing machines, and I only wish for the window, the height, the communion with the natural world, to make what was so uninspired feel like the watershed it was supposed to be.

I WAS CHOSEN.

A tall, blue-eyed, dark-haired man had chosen me. He had moved out of his girlfriend's house and stepped down as the advisor for the student clubs I led. This guitar-playing man, whom others found handsome and desirable, slept in bed beside me, called me pet names, gave me flowers for no reason. Wanted me.

And he wanted others too. First, Heidi. Thin, sexy Heidi, my friend. September of my senior year, eight months after we had been dating, I learned Steven had been sleeping with Heidi for almost as long. Often he left my apartment late at night and drove to hers. He told me that he loved me and wanted to be with me at the same time he was planning a life with her. He would grow angry and yell at me whenever I would question how he danced with her, how he fitted his body into hers, how much time they spent together. His rants would make me feel shallow and unsophisticated. After all, he drank vodka gimlets. I needed to be more broad-minded.

IN OCTOBER WE were engaged.

I can hardly see the girl that was me, this twenty-one-year-old who did not have the strength to leave this man. She had run from so much more, so much less. But she was determined to make this relationship work. His infidelity, if known by others, would reveal her unworthiness, so she kept his secret for him, put it in a drawer, and locked it.

80

The Phone Call

My mother wore black to my wedding. A choice that proved provident as the divorce would take place three and a half years later, but one that, at the time, I found horrifying, even aggressive. My mother's hat was black, as well, with a brim so broad that it extended past her shoulders, helping to keep the Hawaiian sun at bay. Dressed for a funeral but elegant all the same, she managed to conceal with makeup the gash across her eye, a result of a box that had fallen off a shelf and hit her in the face the day before. My mother's wound would not show in the pictures taken by the military photographer hired by my father, but I would always know that just beneath the beige foundation her forehead throbbed in pain. Neither of my parents were pleased.

My mother was not the only one in my family who spent that day in August 1991 hurt and bleeding. My brother Bryan's body also bore scars, another brush with fire, though I could not blame Pele but instead must consider the anger passed down in my family. Two months before I walked down the aisle wearing a dress with a train that unfurled like a fairy tale, Bryan had an accident with a Drano bomb, leaving a furrow of scars on his face and chest that fissured and cracked like lava cooling near the sea.

He and his friend had been making bombs while my parents worked downtown in mirrored buildings that reflected the sky. Small bombs at first, big enough to decapitate a frog but nothing more. Late in the day, boredom set in and the two decided to build a giant bomb inside a Gallo wine jug, the kind with thick green glass and a handle as thick as a thumb. The Drano hummed and sizzled inside, foaming and brewing, trapped in the capped jug, and Bryan realized with a start that this bomb was actually dangerous. Standing on a jetty near the shore of Kailua Bay where they had been tossing bombs all afternoon, he heaved the bottle at the exact moment it exploded. Shards of glass entered his face, neck, and torso, tearing holes in his skin and diving toward his heart. Because he knew my father would be furious, he walked his bleeding body to his friend's house, got into the bathtub, and tried to clean the mess. His friend called the ambulance, amid Bryan's protests, when the bathwater became so bloody he could no longer see the porcelain.

On my wedding day, glass was working its way out of Bryan's body, emerging every few days at his throat or cheek, poking from beneath his skin, causing him to bleed anew. That day, he hid from photographers, volunteered for any job that took him from the crowd, and watched from the side as his sister took the name of a man he had only met once before.

Do I remember a moment, standing with my father outside the dark wooden doors to the church, the winds that had blown my whole life now lifting my veil and swirling it about my knees, when I knew what I was doing was a mistake? Or is that hindsight that makes me think I always knew how it would end?

When Steven called my father and asked his permission to marry me, my father put him on hold. He called my mother at work.

"Is there anything we can do?" he must have asked her.

"No, we will just have to hope she says no."

A week later I called my mother and told her I was engaged.

81

The Bed

They call it the BOGT—the Bed of Good Thoughts—and they run to it every afternoon when they get home from work. She leaves her sandals at the door of their apartment, drops her bag full of worksheets completed by her seventh graders, and takes a flying leap onto the bed. He joins her there, the light coming in through the curtainless windows, traffic far below.

On the BOGT, they lie on their sides and look at each other. He sings a song he has invented about being the Muffin Man.

"I am the Muffin Man, the Muffin Man," he trills.

It makes no sense at all, but she laughs.

"I mix them in the morning before you wake. Bring them to you steaming having just been baked."

They invent names for everything in their lives—their car, their bed, the meals they eat, even each other. He calls her Moo-shu Pork, rarely "Jennifer." Such fictions are important to him. It's why he tells people that he went to the University of Wisconsin and never adds the part about it being the regional campus at Stout. It's not a lie really, more an omission.

On the BOGT, they do not complain about the adolescents they work with or the administrators who seem power hungry and unethical. Instead, he sings about the Muffin

Man. Sometimes he plays his guitar. Entire evenings can pass on the bed, the colors of sunset unnoticed and then gone.

One Friday afternoon, they lie together on the BOGT. Parent/teacher conferences have just ended that day, and she is exhausted.

"Let's go to the happy hour," he says to her. "See people."

But she doesn't want to go. She wants to stay on the BOGT and sing. Or she wants to buy Cinnabons and eat them without forks so their hands become sticky brown messes and their tongues cramp from the sugar. Or she wants to take a long walk in no particular direction and wait to see what they find. She doesn't want to be around people from work, other teachers and their husbands, gathering at a bar eating chips and drinking beer.

It's not that she doesn't want the chips or beer. Being with him, spending all of her time with him, has meant that she eats these things now. Cinnabons and McDonald's biscuits with egg and cheese. He loves food. She loves him. No, her reasons for wanting to stay on the bed have little to do with calories yet everything to do with control. If they remain on the BOGT, they won't have to be around others. Around other women.

"I want to stay home," she says, but he is already pulling on his jeans, patting his hair in the mirror over their dresser.

"We never go out." And she understands this to be her fault. "Come on. Get your shoes."

She will go. She knows this, even as she folds the comforter over her and feels the warmth he has left. She will put her sandals back on and find her purse and maybe wet her brown hair a bit before redrying it. They will drink beer and eat chips and spend their Friday in the bar of a chain restaurant. And he will flirt with the other women, who, in turn, will flitter and bounce. The One He Will Leave Her For will laugh at every story, touch him on the arm. You are so lucky, they say. And for the first two years of their marriage she will think that this is true. Because she and he have the Muffin Man and the BOGT and a car with a license plate bearing both their initials. He calls her Moo Shu and writes her songs and plans for trips to China and Russia that they will never take.

82

The Phone Call

When Steven woke me three years into our marriage and told me that he no longer loved me—like he might tell me that he was too hot or had a stomachache—I was stunned to the point that I did not even cry and actually went back to sleep. In the morning, I had to ask him if he really had said he wanted to leave me as it felt like our conversation had been a dream. Then I got in the shower, chose some clothes, and drove with him to the private school where we both worked. It would take several years before I understood that Steven had left me long before that fall night.

I would not go easily. For six months, we tried counseling. The therapist told me in no uncertain terms that Steven did not love me and that I needed to walk away. For the length of a school year, we pretended to be happily married in front of our friends and family, even though he never touched me. And there were long, tearful conversations where I tried to understand how love unraveled. Each week I got down on my knees in front of him and asked if he had returned to loving me yet. Had the new guitar, the amp, the Hallmark cards, the food, the treats, the trips to the outer islands, the willingness to let him do anything he wanted persuaded him that I was lovable again? Could I change my clothes, my job, the way I ate? Could we start again on the mainland, in Wisconsin, near his friends?

One night, we sat on the balcony of our apartment on the thirty-eighth floor overlooking downtown Honolulu where another day had ended; the sun had long set. I was twenty-four, a year younger than Steven was when I met him. Twin lights on the top of Diamond Head winked in the distance and planes overhead blinked their response. Our chairs sat on opposite sides of the balcony with nothing in between them. Sometimes the trades came up and filled the emptiness with wind. When I put my bare feet to the floor, the AstroTurf reminded me that I was far from the ground.

"I just don't love you," he said, words that floated from his lips only to get eaten by the night. This high up sound came slowly if at all, so the silence was close like cotton. They were the first words he had spoken in an hour.

"Not at all?" I asked.

"Maybe like a sister."

I pulled my legs to my chest, felt the familiar panic rise in my body. I cast about frantically for something I could do or say to keep him here.

"I called my parents today from the pay phone down in the lobby."

I turned my head to face him in the dark.

He continued, "They bought me a ticket home."

For a moment, I was confused. We *were* home, sitting here on our balcony where we could see the Pacific wrap the island in an embrace.

"I fly out on March 5."

He was leaving.

AND HE DID. On our last night together we had dinner at our favorite Thai restaurant. The tables were covered in pink tablecloths with silverware that gleamed in the candlelight. Earlier I had given him a care package filled with presents to make the transpacific flight more bearable—magazines, candy, a new game for his Gameboy that I had spent hours choosing as if it were a diamond. I had packed his suitcases, shipped boxes, and checked the bathroom to make sure he had his razor. During dinner I talked about the Packers and what kind of season they might have. I did whatever I could to make his trip easier in hopes he would change his mind. Or maybe to give me something to focus on besides the fact that I had failed.

AFTER STEVEN BOARDED the plane in March, I returned to our empty apartment and called my parents. Though Steven and I had moved to Hawaii to live near my family, my family had moved back to the mainland within months of our arrival and once again an ocean separated us. The middle of the night in Texas where they now lived, my father was up. I could hear the tinkling of ice in a glass and imagined him pacing the living room with his bourbon and water as we talked. He knew I would call that night. I sat on the floor in my apartment, some four hundred feet from the ground, thousands of miles from the continent, listening to the list of things I needed to do—cancel credit cards, close checking accounts, sell the car—but too tired to find a pen.

"What did I do wrong?" I asked my father, tears coming again as I thought about climbing into the bed alone. Maybe I could sleep on the couch.

My father sighed, began to speak, stopped, and then started again. "You didn't do anything wrong, Jennifer. The relationship ended long before any of this."

"Maybe we should have moved back to the mainland. Or maybe we should have stayed in Nebraska." My mind raced through other possibilities, what I could have done better.

"It's not your fault," he said. "You know that, don't you?"

But I didn't believe him. I knew if I thought hard enough, I could find the answer, the reason my husband now found me intolerable. I knew I was to blame, could feel the weight of that fact sitting on my chest.

"I just feel so sorry for him. When he left tonight, he said he didn't have any keys. Keys to the car, keys to the house. I feel so sorry for him."

My father was silent. I could hear him breathing, hear ice in his glass.

Finally he spoke. "Jennifer, you were perfect in an imperfect relationship."

And even though I knew it wasn't accurate, could name a million ways that I had failed, I thought of what he was saying. My father thought me perfect.

83

The Video

A few years ago, my uncle Keith emailed me a video he had taken during my college years. Because my parents lived so far away, my aunt and uncle often served as surrogate parents at campus events. Which was why, the fall of my senior year when I was on the Homecoming Court, they drove to Lincoln and attended the lunch for parents and then the homecoming game itself before taking me out to dinner. The video is short, less than a minute, and shows my Aunt Joline pinning a corsage onto my dress. The dress is cream and fits tight around my waist before flaring in a circle of fabric below my knees. Wind blows my shoulder-length hair. You can't hear the conversation; there isn't much. We laugh as Joline arranges the flowers against my shoulder. Maybe we recall other past moments involving corsages or pins or flowers still damp from the refrigerator. Someone passes by, outside the frame of the camera, and I nod to them, know them, smile my pleasure at seeing them. It is a warm smile, a confident one.

Today, so many years later, looking at the video clip of this girl, a woman really, but also this girl that was me, I do not recognize myself. She is pretty. Her hair shines in the sun, making me want to touch it, know how it feels. She has been chosen—by a committee or a vote or somehow—to be on the Homecoming Court along with women who are popular and beautiful, women she can never hope to be included with and yet somehow has been. Her dress is well chosen, the cream a good color for her complexion, the style sophisticated. Maybe to those who pass by, those who maybe know her from one of the campus groups she is part of or the Greek system or her work with the Nebraska Humanities Council, the scene makes sense. Everything fits.

And I am shocked, all these years later. Because I know how I felt at that moment, that clear day in October, how I hated my dress, felt out of place with the other attendants, was sure that my escort, a Sig Ep named Jason, was embarrassed that he had to ride in the car with me, stand on the football field with me, hold his arm out for me, when the other women were so thin, so beautiful, so fun to be around, how that was the same month I first learned that Steven had been cheating on me, that I was not enough for him.

My memories do not match the video. The story I have clung to so tightly from birth, of being unchosen, unworthy, is shaken by one minute of film. Memory slips and falters. Can there ever be only one story of the past? It's as if I have been doubled, split in two, only this time I have suffered no concussions. My eyes align. What multiplies are the selves before me, the cowgirl, the girl in the bushes, the one who is thrown in the shower and the one who resists, the pretty one, the angry one, the one who loves her father and the one who fears him, the one who fails in her marriage and gets back up again and runs. She is both sought and lonely. Perfect and failed. Just like her parents. All are caught on video, one autumn day in Nebraska, the wind just lifting the hem of her dress.

84

The Water

The Hawaiian sun sinks into the ocean, carpeting the water in soft pinks and oranges. I am standing on the shores of Ala Moana Beach Park with my friend Kate and her mother. Warm water swirls about our ankles, the surrounding beach empty of tourists and families and the homeless who gather under the palms. In twenty minutes, it will be dark, but for now the sea and the sky are all light and color.

Kate are I are twelve and attend the same school. Her mother has taken us to the grassy beach park for some kind of work event. Hours earlier we had eaten manapua and chicken katsu from lunch trucks, polished off can after can of guava juice. My fingertips are sticky from the day, the corners of my mouth, stiff. We had come to the water to rinse our hands before heading home.

Waves shush to shore and shorebirds dart in and out of the foam. The beat of the waves is steady, like the heart. Standing in the water, sun turned liquid at my feet, I do not want to go, do not want the day to end.

Kate must feel the same way because she turns to her mother, asks, "Can we swim?"

I know it is a fruitless question. We are fully clothed and have no swimsuits.

Her mother looks at her, brow wrinkled, the word "no" already on her lips.

"Please," Kate begs. And then points to the water. My eyes follow her fingers, as must her mother's, and we look at a fleet of clouds outlined in gold, skimming the surface of a sea that holds the color the sky can no longer contain.

"Sure," her mother says. "For a minute."

And with that, we are released into water warmed from the day. We wade out past our shins, past our knees, to our thighs, and then sink beneath the surface. I kneel on the sandy bottom, where the water starts to cool, the light fail.

I am swimming in the ocean fully clothed. I wear the turquoise jumper my mother made me, with a flock of flowers embroidered at the neck. The water pours into the sides of the jumper, beneath my shirt, under the press of my underwear. Soon every part of my body is wet, nothing untouched by the sea. When I surface, I turn on my back and float on the orange water; cooling air brushes my forehead and nose. The ocean rocks me ever closer to the shore, the push and pull of gentle waves, the ferrying of light.

I am not allowed to swim without a bathing suit, without a towel, without the sun to dry my skin before getting into the car. I am not allowed in the water after dark, without a lifeguard, too soon after eating a meal. I cannot swim in my clothes, my underwear, my gold belt even.

And yet, I am.

85

The Hero

The conference begins in Washington, D.C., on Monday; if he takes the red-eye out of Honolulu Friday evening, he should be to Lincoln by the time the ceremony begins. He checks no luggage, carries only a ginger lei in a square plastic box. What he doesn't consider is weather. Who would in May? When he lands in Denver Saturday morning at six a.m., the blizzard rages all around. He cannot see the other planes through the window. If he could, they would not be moving. All flights cancelled. He will not get to Lincoln in time.

SHE IS UPSTAIRS getting ready. The blow dryer circulates the smell of the flowers her parents sent her earlier that morning. A tropical mix that reminds her of home. In two hours, she will give a speech at the Honors Convocation. One of five valedictorians graduating this year, she auditioned to be the one to give the remarks. As she dries her hair, she glances down at the pages in her hand.

SNOW PILES ON the runway, clouds gather grey and pregnant with more. He begs the flight attendant to find him a seat on another airline.

"Everything is shut down, sir," she responds. "No one is going anywhere."

As far as he can see in every direction, the sky stretches leaden. Somewhere to the right are the mountains. Somewhere to the left, the daughter he cannot get to.

"PHONE CALL, JENNIFER."

She zips her dress and puts on her heels before walking the two flights of stairs to the phone. Who would be calling her this early in the morning?

"Hello?"

"Hi, Jennifer."

"Hey, Dad. What are you doing?"

"Ruining a surprise," he says. He had wanted to watch her give her honor's speech, but he was stuck in Denver and would fail to get there on time.

"I'm sorry," he says. And tears gather in her eyes because she has lost what she didn't even know she had.

"It's okay," she tells him. "It's okay, Dad."

AT EIGHT IN the morning, the skies part like the Red Sea itself, and the sun shines down on the blanket of snow. He had been sleeping in a chair with the lei on his lap.

"Now boarding Flight 8517 to Lincoln."

His will be one of only a handful of flights to make it out of Stapleton that morning. When he lands in Lincoln, twenty minutes before the Honors Convocation begins, the snows will have followed him.

SHE SITS ON the stage with the president of the university and some distinguished alumni. Several thousand parents, relatives, professors, and friends flank those being honored that morning. She rolls her five-page speech in her hand and waits for her name to be called. Somewhere out there, she knows her aunt and uncle sit, as well as her fiancé. Her father, though, is not among them. The only place he exists at this moment is in her words.

She chose to speak about her father, long, long before she knew he was going to try and come. She has written about how he used to tickle her in the ocean where her feet couldn't touch bottom, and how he would chant the whole time, "Giggle and drown. Giggle and drown."

It was a lesson in remaining focused, on being strong. At some point, amid the choking, gasping, and laughing, she would always save herself. Her speech that morning is about the gift her father gave her—the strength to do the hard thing. As a valedictorian in a school of thousands, far, far from home, she has, it seems, proven her ability to do just that.

WHEN HE LEAVES the doors of the tiny Lincoln airport, he sees only one cab. In the swirling snow, he knows no others will be along anytime soon.

Leaning into the window of the cab, he asks the driver if he can take him to the university.

"I'm waiting for someone," the cabbie responds.

"Who?"

"I can't remember the name," the driver responds, "someone meeting his daughter."

"That's me," my father says. "That's me."

THE PRESIDENT IS finishing his remarks. Soon she will be called. She wants to do a good job, make her parents proud of her, reassure them that she is okay, even though they will not be here to witness the moment. What she cannot say that morning, holding her father's story in her hands, is that what she is really describing in her speech is not just what it takes to stay afloat, but the miracle of breathing at all. Because when her father tickled her and she took the sea into her nose and throat, she was, yes, terrified, but also fully present. The sky vaulted above her, the amniotic waters held her, and she turned her attention to the most ordinary of acts, breathing in and breathing out. What was ordinary became marked and necessary. It was given its place. Terrifying, exhilarating, all at once. There in the ocean, under the sun, scared and laughing, she was alive.

THE COLISEUM HAS changed since he was on campus several decades ago. Instead of one entrance, there are many.

"Which door do you want?" the cabbie asks.

"I have no idea," the man responds. "You choose."

AS SHE SITS waiting, a young man suddenly walks across the stage in front of the president, who has not finished his speech. The president follows him with his eyes but does not pause. The young man approaches her and takes something from his hands. It is a ginger lei, the gift you give in the islands to say hello and good-bye and I love you. The young man places it around her neck. The flowers are heavy and fragrant. Her father is there.

86

The Bucket

The morning after Steven leaves, I wake on the BOGT. March sunlight floods the bedroom revealing the layer of dust that has accumulated atop the pressed-board dresser. Out the window: sky. Diamond Head glows green in the distance, its volcanic top like the prow of a ship headed out to sea. Below, the world marches by in miniature, unaware that I have been left. The phone still sits on the bed, Kleenex balled in tiny fists around my head; the room looks the same as it did the night before. I move my arms against the white sheets, feel the polyester grab at the tiny hairs on my arms. I am here. Steven is gone. I remain.

I make coffee and take a shower. Steven's razor is gone, but my shampoo and conditioner sit on the edge of the tub. When I go to find clothes to wear, I slide open my side of the closet, leaving his closed. My clothes hang there as they always have. They fit the same. So do my shoes. I pull a sundress over my head, find some sandals to wear, and head for the balcony. The morning sun warms me as I stand with my coffee at the rail. The sky stretches beyond Diamond Head, keeping the ocean company for thousands of miles. I can make out tiny sailboats on the horizon, a few pigeons flying just below me. Though I can't see them, I imagine people stand on the shore of the beach, early morning walkers, shell hunters, those who have yet to go to bed. They all have buckets of their own.

Years after the Winnie trip, I asked my parents what they remembered of the summer. Both responded that it was a great trip, a wonderful time in our lives, the trip, in fact, my dad had always envisioned. My mother remembered laughing across the country as the Winnie fell apart and the rains came down. It made me wish I had been in their Winnebago.

But their Winnie was not my Winnie. In my Winnie, no one steered. We careened madly down the road by day and left spinning cars in our wake. Tires exploded like bombs, matched in ferocity only by tempers. And each morning we emerged, sometimes in the sun and sometimes in the rain, and ate cold cereal on a table that had moments ago been my bed. And yet, there we all are, breathing in unison just before dawn. It seems there were at least two Winnies on the road that summer just like there had been two women standing in the October sun on homecoming weekend. Multiple versions of the same story. As you hold the plywood against the frame of the garage while your father pounds nails, you are laughing or you are crying or you are doing both.

What one sees as a miracle, another terms sacrifice. What one sees as broken, another, whole.

THE DAY MOVES forward as I remain on the balcony overlooking Waikiki. My coffee cools in the morning air. Soon I will leave the apartment and lock the door, double-checking the dead bolt as I always do. And then I will take the stairs rather than the elevator and wait to the last minute to fill up my gas tank in hopes that gas prices will magically drop. I will spend too long trying to find the best parking spot and think of my father the whole time I hunt. I will teach my students Latinate suffixes and bribe them with candy and cupcakes and praise. And then I will come home.

Sounds begin to sift up to me from the street below, a car alarm, a horn, two dogs barking at each other from passing cars. I stand in the muffled sound and look again to the edge of the island, the deep blue of the Pacific pinned like a quilt all around.

Then I take my place beside the others whom I cannot see on the shore. Foam swirls at our shins, bubbles popping in the air. When I see the cowrie roll past my feet, its lip broken but its colors undimmed, I pick it up, feel its slick shell, the fissure of its lips, then place it in my bucket. Later, I add firework-shaped seaweed and the bottom of a cone shell, worn smooth by its journey. The buckets carried by those around me, I note, are full as well. Our feet sink deeper into the sand, the spaces between our toes growing cool, the waves beating a steady rhythm all around us. Neither fully on shore nor at sea, we wait for the sun to warm our bodies, for the gulls to call our names.

87

The Birth

In 2004, my first son, Aidan, was born by a vacuum, a fierce plastic instrument that sucked him from my body, his head bearing a red ring for days. I had held him inside, knowing the connection between birthing and breaking, thinking I could keep him safe somehow. As my body tried to push him out, part of me struggled to have him remain. I saw the intrusion of the doctor as a rebuke. A stronger woman would not have required the intervention.

With my second son, two years later, I tried again. The labor was faster this time; my body knew the rhythms of birth, the surges that move like waves across the sea. I remember thinking in the parking lot of the hospital as another contraction forced me to lean against the car and threatened to bring me to my knees that I didn't have to do this again. I could ask for drugs. Drugs that would block the pain, numb my body, cause me to forget. The idea that I did have choices reassured me, even as I knew I wanted to do it on my own. It took me a half hour to walk from the parking lot to the front desk, stopping every few minutes while my body turned inward.

Hours into the labor, the midwife broke my water. It was Mother's Day and she wanted to be home with her family. A faster labor was better for her, and, she argued, better for me. In my worn state, I agreed. Within seconds of piercing the amniotic sac—the sea inside me rushing out, warm and wet, meeting my thighs and the bed beneath me—the need to push became insurmountable. And I became the animal that I am.

"Jennifer, you are resisting," Deb, the midwife, said. "You are fighting your body."

From my mouth, no, from my body came sounds I could not have imagined I could make. Moans, deep, guttural, noises not my own. For a minute I worried I would scare my husband, Michael, scare the nurses, that they would leave me because they could no longer recognize me, because I embarrassed them, because I would not keep quiet, be polite, use my indoor voice. I closed my eyes.

Other women have said that birth is not painful, and they are right. What your body experiences belongs to another realm. It is totalizing. You are the birth. You are your body. Nothing else. You cannot step away, take a break, reconsider. You, as you have always thought of you, cease to exist.

I had a choice. Even as the contractions consumed me, I knew I had a choice. And I remember making the decision to go into the pain, to hand my body over to it, let it break me, halve me, leave me destroyed. I will let go, I thought. Not because I wanted to do it "right," not because I recalled failing with my first son, but because I wanted to see if I would survive. For the first time in my life, I wanted to trust a body, my body, the one that refused to be controlled, the one that had betrayed me, grown hair, bled, and peed, the one that I had starved, the one rejected by Steven, the one I had kept covered and contained for so many years, and see if that body would hold.

So I dove down, riding the next contraction into oblivion. Deeper and deeper I dove, searching for the heart of the pain, the beginning place. I swam past my brother lying on the bottom of the pool, his hair waving like seaweed in the wake of my kick, his disposable diapers bloated with chlorinated water, past the pocket I knew could never keep me safe, safe no longer even seemed like a reasonable concept, a thing worth seeking, laughable, past the bottom, the coral, the reef, the sandy floor, past the scalding water searing Bryan's, no George's, no Bryan's newborn skin, the nurse already gone, fire licking at his ankles, his thighs, the tiny curve of his bottom, past the marlin, sides beaten to a pulp, eye shattered like the ice on a pond just before it gives way, past the broken records, broken heads, broken treaties, broken promises—the one to keep you safe, the one till death do you part, the one not to eat that brownie, that pie, that peanut butter sandwich—until I heard the screams, and then I stopped. I was in a hole, a cave really, though my eyes were closed, so I could only imagine this place, hear the place, hear the crying, the suffering, a language all its own, my father, ten years old, as he hammers his pet pig, the wail inside his small body as he drowns the cats, fights the bullies, holds a man's severed hand in his own, the scream of my mother, her son cold and wet against her body, no breath, no movement, her sky-shattering cries that cause the crows to bolt from the limbs, he is dead, the pleas of my aunt as her father rapes her, splits her body open like a pomegranate, the cries of my aunt as her father-in-law enters her, the moans of my cousins as their grandpa forces himself into their tiny bodies, and, too, the cries of my grandpa, twelve, sold by his own mother, sold for a few dollars into slavery, on a train that will take him into the earth where he will forget how to see, and other cries, those I don't recognize at all, but insistent, cries without stories, or stories I haven't heard, stories not my own, a chorus of suffering, melding into one, and then, quieter, but still there, still there, amid all that pain, all that torment, the cries of a baby, left in a bucket, broken and blue, I am not dead, she wails, I am not dead. I am not dead. I am not dead.

And that is it. What I had never realized before, never considered, would not have known had I not found myself at the center of things: she wanted to live. She wanted to live. I realize at that moment she wanted to live. She wanted to come into this world full of pain, with absence the constant, and loss everywhere, but also full of moments where the ocean glints beneath the sun, the world cracks open in a display of color and light, and her father makes it to the coliseum on time, moments when her skin tingles, her hair shines, her mother smiles, and she eats dinner spinning through the sky. She wanted all of it. She, not her father or her mother or the doctor who stooped to peer inside the bucket, forced herself into this spinning world, joining the lives of her parents and her siblings, willing to barter loss against love, and persevere. She wanted all of it. The dead baby breathes.

Acknowledgments

This book has been in the making for well over a decade. In fact, the first story I ever drafted for Ordinary Trauma I wrote in 1998 as a doctoral student in Ruth Behar's Experimental Ethnography course at the University of Michigan. At the time, I was just playing with language and form, thinking about the place of stories in our lives. Twenty years later, I have come to understand how the past is a key to the present—how a story, the way we shape a story, tells us little about then and everything about now. In this way, writing memoir makes us more compassionate—toward ourselves and others. I have long told my students that the world would be a better place if we all had to find the stakes in our past. I also understand, most intimately, the labor of craft. The work writing takes. Anyone who suggests the process is anything other than painful and difficult is lying.

It can be joyful too, of course, but that joy usually arises from the companionship offered by those willing to gather around the work rather than the turn of a line. I have been helped by so many, more than I could possibly name here. Yet, I will try.

My thanks to John Alley and the University of Utah Press for their support of the project. He believed in it from the very beginning and his faith has never wavered.

I have also had the great good fortune of being part of a writing group in Logan, Utah, informally known as Splinters. The membership has changed over the past thirteen years, but everyone in that group has helped bring this book into being. My thanks, then, to Chris Cokinos, Kathe Lison, Charles Waugh, Michael Sowder, Maria Melendez, Ben Gunsberg, and the late Ken Brewer. Their love and friendship has been as essential as their guidance. I am grateful also to Dinty W. Moore and Debra Gwartney. Their lyrical writing has been an inspiration and their feedback and support, invaluable. Kathe Lison, Morgan Sanford, and Millie Tullis helped make the final manuscript as strong as it could be. Rona Kaufman is one of two people in my life who has been with this project since 1998 and has, many, many times, refused to allow me to quit, willed me to try again.

I am forever grateful to my family, my parents and my brothers, Scott and Bryan. They never asked to be in this book. The story they would tell about the bomb shelter or the swimming pool or the time we drove a Winnie through Boston at rush hour would be markedly different than the one I have told here. Versions of the past only make our lives richer. I am so thankful for their love. It is in their hearts that I grew into the person that I am. To my sons, as well, Aidan and Kellen. Nothing made the past more clear and precious to me than being a mother to these two open-hearted boys. I rise to meet them.

Lastly and most dearly, my deep and abiding gratitude to my husband, Michael, who called me a writer long before I could call myself one. He knows every word in this book as well as I do. More importantly, he has taught me how to love this world and to believe in the abundance it offers. To quote Hafiz: "A love like that lights the whole sky."